PORTRAITS OF
AFRICA

PORTRAITS OF
AFRICA

MOHAMED AMIN

Text by Peter Moll

Harvill Press
8 Grafton Street
London W1

Acknowledgments

We wish to record our thanks to the very many individuals and organisations who have assisted over the years in making possible the series of journeys across Kenya on which this book is based, especially to Dr Anne Spoerry and Sister Sean Underwood of AMREF/EA Flying Doctors Service; the late Father Joseph Polet and the late Father Louis Graiff (who gave their lives in the service of the nomads of Northern Kenya); Father Redento Tignosini and the Consolata Fathers of the Diocese of Marsabit; James de Vere Allen and Omari Bwana, MP, for their assistance in the Lamu archipelago; Dr Rachel Masake for help on the Iteso; Charles Njonjo, MP, for assisting our coverage of the Kikuyu; John Arunga of the Department of Fisheries, Kisumu; Moses Mayo Lenairoshi of the Samburu County Council and Chief Simon Peter Lekarikei of Maralal.

Thanks are also due to the librarians of The British Institute, Nairobi, the McMillan Library of the Nairobi City Council, the University of Nairobi and the Institute of African Studies and to Alison Abell who obtained for the authors many of the reference books listed in the bibliography. The research assistance of Humphrey Kimaru Kariuki was invaluable. We record our appreciation to Dr Bethwell Ogot, Dip.Ed. (East Africa), MA (St Andrews), Ph.D. History (London), President of the International Scientific Committee for the UNESCO General History of Africa; Chris Wanjala, BA (Hons), Ph.D. Litt. (Nairobi), Acting Director of the Institute of African Studies at the University of Nairobi; and to Ian Parker for reading the manuscript in its first draft and for their valued and pertinent comments. Deborah Shepherd and Brian Tetley's editing of the manuscript is gratefully acknowledged and special thanks are due to Sarah Gichuhi and Joyce Mbao for typing field notes and the manuscript.

We are grateful to Dr Bernd Heine and Dr W. Mohlig of the University of Cologne for permission to adapt their language map of Kenya and to Mohamed Akbar for specially producing the maps.

The spelling of place-names follows that laid down in the Kenya Gazetteer produced by the Survey of Kenya. The use of kilometres for distance and metres for height is the official policy in Kenya.

Harvill Press Ltd is a subsidiary company of William Collins Sons & Company Limited

London · Glasgow · Sydney · Auckland Toronto · Johannesburg

British Library Cataloguing in Publication Data

Amin, Mohamed
  Portraits of Africa.
  1. Kenya—Description and travel
  I. Title   II. Moll, Peter
  916.76'02044   DT433.527

ISBN 0–00–272639 4

First published in the United Kingdom by Harvill Press, 1983

©Camerapix 1983

This book was designed and produced by Camerapix Publishers International, P.O. Box 45048, Nairobi, Kenya

Designed by Craig Dodd

Filmset in Great Britain by Keyspools Ltd, Golborne, Lancs
Printed in Italy by Arnoldo Mondadori Editore, Verona

Contents

Introduction

Kenya is a microcosm of Africa: an area inhabited by all three of the great language families of the continent. There are many books on Kenya, but none that comprehensively or adequately portrays the lifestyles and history of its people. *Portraits of Africa* is intended to make good that deficiency. It provides a concise and perceptive insight into the customs and cultures of the ethnic groups that constitute the independent nation of Kenya and, in a more universal way, an appreciation of the interaction and values of the people of Africa.

We are indebted to Dr Bernd Heine and Dr W. Mohlig of the University of Cologne for the basis of classification by language used throughout this work. With the exception of those spoken by recent immigrant communities, the languages of Kenya can be divided into three distinct genetic groupings, Bantu, Nilotic and Cushitic. Each of these groups belongs to a different language family – the Bantu to the Niger–Kordofanian family, Nilotic to the Nilo–Saharan family and Cushitic to the Hamito–Semitic family of Afro–Asiatic origin.

Within Kenya the Bantu languages are further classified geographically into Western, Central and Eastern. The Nilotic languages are divided into three branches, Western, Eastern and Southern although Maa, an Eastern Nilotic language, is spoken far south of any Southern Nilotic language. The Cushitic languages are represented in Kenya by two different branches, the Eastern and Southern Cushitic (Dahalo being the sole example of the latter still spoken in Kenya).

Bantu			Cushitic		Nilotic		
Western	Central	Coastal	Eastern	Southern	Western	Southern	Eastern
Gusii	Embu	Bajun	Boni	Dahalo	Luo	(Kalenjin)	(Ateker)
Kuria	Kamba	Mijikenda	Boran			Keiyo	Iteso
Luyia	Kikuyu	Pokomo	Burji			Kipsigis	Turkana
Suba	Mbeere	Segeju	Dassa-			Marakwet	(Maa)
	Meru	Shirazi	nich			Nandi	Ilchamus
	Taita	Swahili	El Molo			Okiek	Maasai
	Taveta		Gabbra			Pokot	Samburu
	Tharaka		Orma			Sabaot	
			Rendille			Tuken	
			Sakuye				
			Somali				
			Wata				
			Yaaku				

Although it is not easy to determine the boundary between a language and a dialect, on the foregoing classification it can be said that some thirty languages are spoken in Kenya. Many languages may be mutually intelligible and decisions as to their status may only be arbitrary and made with many reservations. Two-thirds of Kenya's people speak a Bantu language as their mother tongue; 30 per cent are Nilotic speakers and only 3 per cent speak Cushitic languages – although the mainly nomadic people of this group range across 40 per cent of the 582,644 square kilometres of Kenya's territory.

One effect of the colonial regime was to make the divisions between tribes more rigid, more distinctive and, therefore, more closely associated with vested interests, rights and privileges. Most early European administrators too readily identified tribes as time-honoured units. But, as linguistic and anthropological studies are continuing to reveal, this was far from the truth and remains so.

Before the arrival of the European, three great waves – the largely but not

7

exclusively agricultural Bantu, the pastoral Cushitic speakers and the pastoral/ agricultural Nilotics – had moved over the centuries into the area now defined as Kenya. Small groups of hunter-gatherers in this then sparsely populated region of Africa were swamped as the conflicting tides of people met, and out of the eddies and whirlpools of their intermingling today's groupings began to develop. Environmental considerations resulted in a further coalescence of interests and cultures and the emergence of the tribes which now occupy the region.

The most succinct, if somewhat inadequate definition we have been able to find for that often misinterpreted word 'tribe' is that provided by Professor P. H. Gulliver. He suggests that 'tribe' can be taken to apply to 'any group of people which is distinguished, by its members and by others, on the basis of cultural-regional criteria'. It is in this sense that the term has been used in this study of Kenya's people, although where possible its use has been avoided. Its substitution by 'ethnic group', with its wider connotations, is not wholly satisfactory.

Inevitably, the terminology of the social anthropologist occurs throughout this study although such words have been avoided where possible. For the sake of clarity, therefore, several terms applied to the various group initiations and stages in the life-cycle of many of Kenya's people need to be defined.

Age-grades are categories or stages into which the life-cycle of the individual is divided according to relative age. These are stages through which each set of initiates passes in succession (for example, among the Maasai that of junior warrior, senior warrior, junior elder, senior elder).

Members of *age-sets* are initiated during the same period on the basis of their approximate age. Each group is organised as an entity, separated from the next group by a closed period during which no initiation takes place. Members share specific rights and obligations to each other, and remain members of the group for as long as it exists.

Generation-sets differ from age-sets by the method of recruitment, being formed on a genealogical basis at regular intervals. Thus all the sons of one man are recruited into a generation-set which occurs some prescribed number of sets after his own. The composition and social function of generation-sets also differ. Many ethnic groups are divided into two sections, each of which is referred to as a moiety.

The names of the ethnic groups are those in common usage. However, the Kiswahili plural prefix 'Wa' (as distinct from the singular prefix 'M') is frequently used by Kenyans when referring to these groups, as in Wakikuyu, Wataita, Wamaasai, Wanandi and so on. The Western Bantu groups incorporate their own plural prefix 'Aba', as in Abaluyia, Abagusii, Abasuba, Abakuria. Ilchamus has been used instead of the more common Itiamus for the people of Lake Baringo; and Oromo, now favoured by modern scholarship, has been adopted throughout for the people of Ethiopia and the Horn of Africa hitherto referred to as the Galla. Population figures are based on the 1979 Kenyan national census.

To attempt to provide, within the limitations of a thousand-word essay, anything but the most superficial appraisal of a complex tribal society and the more interesting aspects of traditional life and customs, kinship and behaviour and economic organisation is clearly hazardous. Each of the following descriptions of the forty or so ethnic groups which make up the people of the Kenya nation must therefore be regarded only as a brief if thorough outline; for brevity, footnotes have been excluded and a comprehensive bibliography of reference sources is provided for those wishing to make a more detailed and scholarly study of Kenya's people.

The authors travelled many thousands of kilometres, by foot, four-wheel-

drive vehicle, plane, raft and canoe on lakes Victoria, Turkana and Baringo, through the Lamu archipelago and along the river Tana. The collection of photographs used as the basis for this work took seven years to assemble, in a series of journeys which criss-crossed Kenya. Many scores of people – missionaries, administrators, teachers, pilots and ordinary folk – showed great kindness and hospitality, often inadequately acknowledged. We hope that this book will justify their assistance and provide a better understanding of the people of Kenya and of the land in which they live.

Mohamed Amin
Peter Moll

Nairobi, Kenya
August 1983

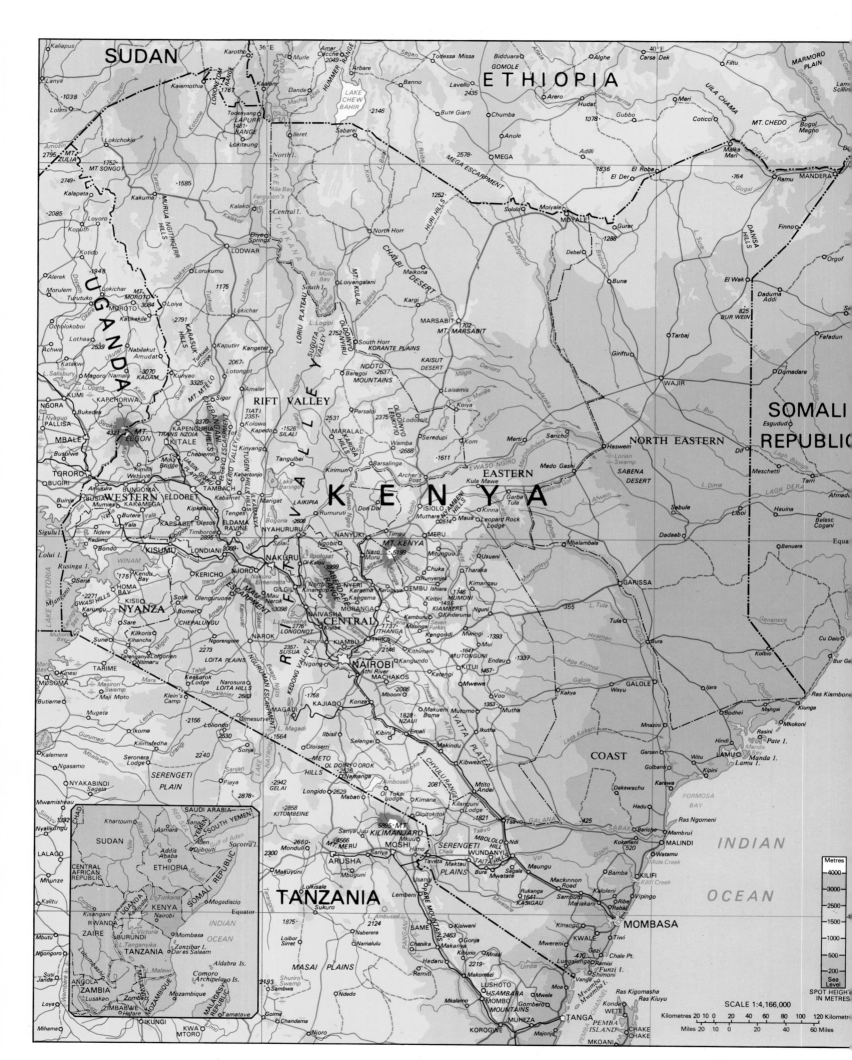

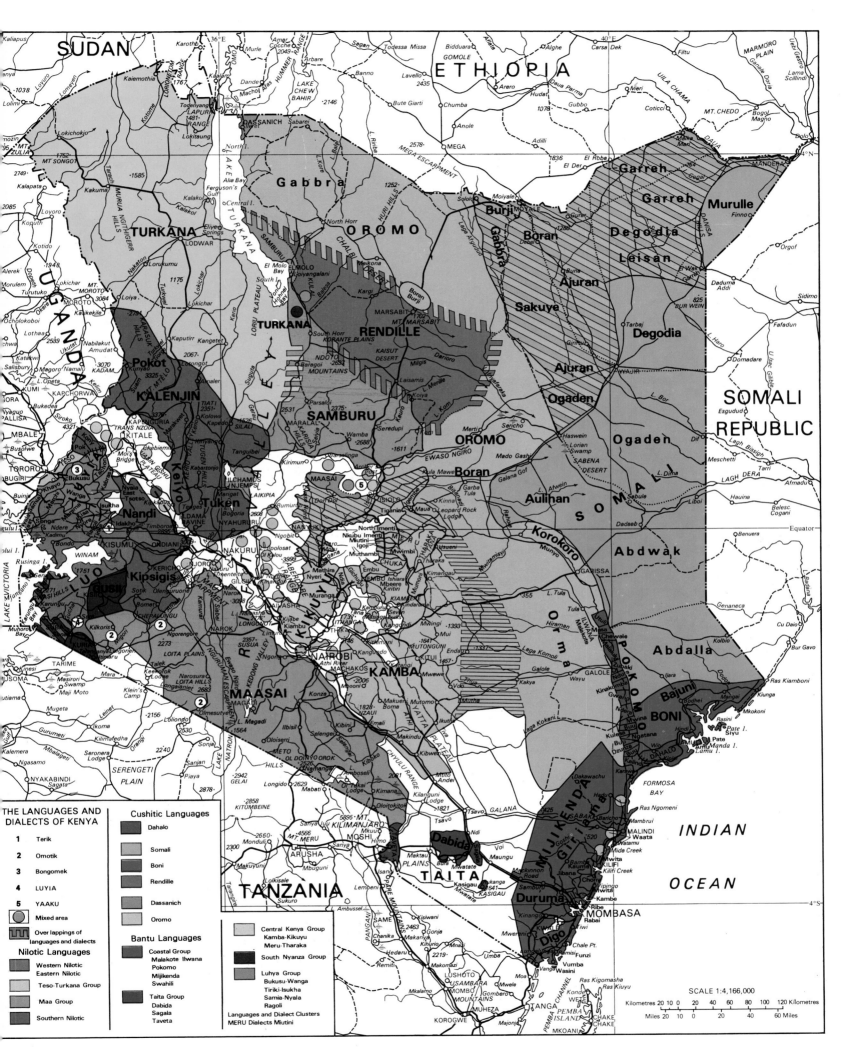

THE LANGUAGES AND
DIALECTS OF KENYA

1   Terik

2   Omotik

3   Bongomek

4   LUYIA

5   YAAKU

⬤   Mixed area

▥   Over lappings of
    languages and dialects

Nilotic Languages

Western Nilotic
Eastern Nilotic

Teso-Turkana Group

Maa Group

Southern Nilotic

Cushitic Languages

Dahalo

Somali

Boni

Rendille

Dassanich

Oromo

Bantu Languages

Coastal Group
  Malakote Ilwana
  Pokomo
  Mijikenda
  Swahili

Taita Group
  Dabida
  Sagala
  Taveta

Central Kenya Group
  Kamba-Kikuyu
  Meru-Tharaka

South Nyanza Group

Luhya Group
  Bukusu-Wanga
  Tiriki-Isukha
  Samia-Nyala
  Ragoli

Languages and Dialect Clusters
MERU Dialects Miutini

SCALE 1:4,166,000

Kilometres 20 10 0   20   40   60   80   100 120 Kilometres

Miles 20   10 0   20   40   60 Miles

Bajun, Swahili, Shirazi
EASTERN BANTU

The Swahili-speaking people of the Kenya coast share a common language, religion (Islam) and culture. Of Bantu origin, Kiswahili (especially the standard Kiunguja of Zanzibar) has become the national language of Kenya and is widely spoken throughout East and Central Africa and Zaire.

The Bajun (37,000) of the Lamu archipelago and coastal strip to the north, and those islands parallel to it, speak a dialect of their own known as Kitikuu – with Kiamu and Kivita, one of more than a dozen forms of Swahili still spoken. Like the Pokomo and the Mijikenda, the Bajun are held to have originated from a homeland in Shungwaya to the north, the exact location of which is as yet undetermined. Arabian settlement from the Hijaz, the Persian Gulf and South Arabia brought about a further evolution of the Bajun people, as did the later Oromo incursions.

The centuries of immigration and conquest, transmigration and miscegenation, resulted in the Bantu-speaking Swahili absorbing immigrants of Arab and Persian descent. Loosely applied, the term Swahili has come to mean almost any Muslim from the coast, but refers specifically to the Wavumba of Vanga and the Wavita of Mombasa. The three tribes (*Thelatha Taifa*) of the Kilindini and the Nine Tribes (*Tissa Taifa*) of the Wavita constituted the Twelve Tribes (*Thenaashara Taifa*) of the Swahili of Mombasa, the original inhabitants of the town.

The Shirazi (numbering, together with the Swahili, 5,500) are a scattered maritime and agricultural people who claim to have originated from a homeland in Persia in the tenth to twelfth centuries and once made up the aristocratic families and dynasties of the Ozi kingdoms of Shaka, Mwana and Ungwana, and Malindi and Mombasa. The modern view places no credence in the legend of their origins and today little remains to set them apart from the Swahili other than a pride in a glorious past.

Fishing and agriculture feature prominently in the economy of the Bajun, Swahili and Shirazi. Fish spears, handlines (*mishipi*) on which *chungu, danfu, kole kole* and *nguru* are caught, several different types of basket traps made of palm rib or split bamboo and weirs are all common methods of catching fish. The fine-meshed cast nets (*kidifu*) used for catching *dagaa*, the drift nets (*majerifa*) employed in surface fishing from boats and the long seine nets (*majuya*) positioned from boats and then hand-hauled up on the beach are employed in communal fishing.

From recorded time, the peoples of the Kenya coast have engaged in shifting agriculture. The bush fires on the mainland, to clear land for planting before the rains, are mentioned in the second-century *Periplus of the Erithrean Sea*. Of considerable importance in the economy is the ubiquitous coconut, which provides the raw material for building and thatching, rope-making and plaited basket work, food, drink and oil. The coastal people cultivate numerous root crops, including cassava (*muhogo*), sweet potato (*kiasi*), yam (*kiasi kikuu*) and taro (*majungwa*); cereals such as millet (*mtama*), rice (*mpunga*) and maize (*mahindi*) and a wide variety of fruit trees including banana (*mgomba* – the fruit is called *ndizi*), mango (*mwembe*), orange (*mchungwa*), lime (*mlimao*) and pawpaw. Cashews, cotton, and mangrove cutting in the Lamu area provide important cash incomes.

The ocean-going dhows (*madau*) used for trade down the East Coast from Arabia, the Persian Gulf and even Pakistan and India still arrive in Lamu, Malindi and Mombasa at the start of the south-west monsoon. Long ago, the dhow fleet numbered several hundred; today only a few individual, motorised dhows maintain these age-old trading links. On the creeks and in the harbours a dug-out canoe (*mtumbwi*) is commonly used and an occasional double-outrigger canoe (*ngalawa*) may also be seen. The graceful *jahazi* with its billowing triangular sail and coconut-matting splash 'boards' is the common

Above: A Bajun girl grooms her younger brother in a moment of family intimacy in Siyu on Pate island, in the Lamu archipelago of Kenya's nothern coast.

Opposite: Islamic insistence on female modesty decreed the all-embracing black buibui *worn by Bajun women of Lamu.*

Below: The exquisitely carved ivory siwa *of Pate dates back to* 1698 *and is one of the most important pieces in the Lamu National Museum. More than two metres long, this musical instrument has two articulated joints. Centuries ago* siwa *were part of the ritual regalia of all Swahili towns. Lamu waterfront is in the background.*

Opposite: The graceful lines of an inshore dhow take shape on a quiet beach in Lamu. Matondoni boatbuilders are fashioning a jahazi, *a common sailing craft of the Lamu archipelago, using* Mn'gambo wood (Manilkara sansibarensis). *Known to the Swahili craftsmen as* miti-chuma, *the wood is obtained from the mainland Witu forest. Seams caulked with cotton strands,* kalafati, *the finished vessel will be launched down a slipway of mangrove poles.*

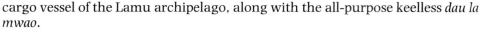

cargo vessel of the Lamu archipelago, along with the all-purpose keelless *dau la mwao.*

Many coast people are skilled craftsmen. Lime burning from coral is still an important industry; ship-building and wood-working, plaiting of baskets, mats and other items, rope-making from coir, and metal and leather work remain traditional occupations of the villagers.

Formerly the coastal strip was a possession of the Sultan of Zanzibar (leased as a protectorate to Great Britain in 1895) and many of the Swahili-speaking community placed higher regard on their affiliations with the Arabs than those with the peoples of the hinterland. Today this stance has been abandoned, and the Bajun, Swahili and Shirazi have integrated as an African people and united with other Kenyans.

Above: In former times tradition demanded that a Swahili noblewoman should not display herself in public and this colourful canopy, the sheraa, *was designed to ensure that her privacy (and her modesty) were not infringed.*

Opposite: Lamu, a devout Muslim community, celebrates the Prophet's Birthday, Maulidi al Nebi, *one of the most important events in the Islamic calendar. Celebrants mark the festival with dances and processions.*

Boni, Wata and Yaaku
EASTERN CUSHITIC

Dahalo
SOUTHERN CUSHITIC

Several small groups of hunter-gatherer peoples still inhabit the hinterland of the coast (Boni, Wata and Dahalo) and, far inland, the Mukogodo massif north of Mount Kenya (Yaaku). There is linguistic, anthropological and other data to suggest that the Boni, Wata and Dahalo are survivors of early hunters who were subsequently widely influenced by and adopted the languages of the Southern and Eastern Cushitic peoples who migrated into the area. The Dahalo, believed to have once spoken a bushman Khosian 'click' language, are said to share ethnic and cultural ties with similar groups in northern Tanzania such as the Tatoga and Iraqw.

The Boni call themselves and speak a language known as Aweer. They were formerly divided into at least a dozen sub-groups, each of which was associated with a particular territory over which it ranged, although individual communication between groups was frequent. They were nomadic and had few permanent settlements. The dry season, when they tended to congregate around the waterholes, was a time of relative stability, in contrast to the constant shifting of the family groups during and after the rains, when one site or another was rarely occupied for more than a few weeks. The pattern of Boni settlement was disrupted in the 1960s by the Shifta (Somali bandit) raids throughout northern Kenya, and the Boni are now grouped at Busuba, Mangai and Mararani and several other small villages located along the Mokowe–Kiunga road.

Their traditional economy was based on hunting and gathering of roots, wild fruits and honey. The Boni (who together with the Wata number over 4,000) had no livestock and cultivated only small plots of sorghum and millet. More recently agriculture has become the main occupation and chickens, goats and occasionally a few cattle are kept. Today, extensive areas are being cleared for cultivation, and sesame, maize, cassava, pumpkin, bananas and pawpaw are grown to augment their traditional diet. But following the rains, family groups of women and children use digging sticks to obtain edible roots and gather berries and fruit from the wild cycad, baobab and other trees. After boiling, drying and grinding the kernels of the cycad are used as flour. Even the pith of the stem may be used as a famine food: the chopped pith is allowed to ferment for a week, then washed in hot water, dried in the sun and pounded to make a flour for porridge. Honey gathering and hunting are the men's tasks. Bows and poisoned arrows, the detachable metal heads of which bear the owner's special mark, are used from hides close to waterholes to kill game, which are tracked until the poison takes full effect. Reputed elephant hunters, the Boni trade ivory with the Somali and the Swahili of Lamu and Witu. Negligible hunting takes place today and is confined to the killing of a few topi, bushbuck and waterbuck for food.

Boni huts are circular domed structures of the 'beehive' type, made from branches and thin saplings tied together and thatched with doum palm leaves. Size depends on the number of occupants. The hut of a widow or a middle-aged woman whose husband has left her may be only three metres in diameter; a family with children will occupy a hut up to five metres in diameter. Unmarried girls may occasionally share a common hut. In contrast, men who have left their wives or whose wives have died, or who are away visiting another group, sleep in the open by a fire. Boni sections are often linked in marriage through the exchange of sisters, making for stability and co-operation.

The Wata, called the Wasanye by the Swahili and Ariangulu (said to mean 'eaters of tortoise') by the Mijikenda, are found from Kipini to beyond the Kenya border with Tanzania and Takaunga to Voi. Wata is also the Oromo name for all hunter-gatherers, irrespective of the territory they occupy. The Wata may have spoken the Dahaloan language of the Southern Cushitic migrants – traces of which might still be found in the Wata technical, hunting-gathering

Above: Long bow at the ready, a Boni elephant hunter takes aim. Strict game laws now forbid this traditional pursuit.

Opposite: Attractive Boni girl relaxes in Bodhei village. Former hunter-gatherers, the group are now settled in permanent communities with increasingly closer ties with the neighbouring Bajun.

Opposite: Wata woodcarvers in Tarasaa, north of Malindi, add the final touches to a consignment of containers, fashioned from raw logs, for sale among th neighbouring Orma with whom they have traded craft and game trophies for centuries.

terminology – before succumbing to more recent Oromo (Eastern Cushitic) influence.

Prominent among the small settlements in which the Wata live is that near Mlango Moro close to Mangea Hill just west of the Arabuko Sokoke forest and at Kilibasi in Coast Province. Even smaller settlements of rarely more than twenty to thirty people are to be found in the surrounding areas. Wata huts are similar to, if smaller than, those of the Boni. More usually they are grass thatched and a grass screen is pulled across the low, one-metre doorway at night. Like the Boni, the Wata are accomplished hunters, using bows up to two metres long to fire a one-metre, iron-barbed poisoned arrow to kill big game, including elephants. The tar-like, black poison is made from an infusion of the roots and bark of the *Acokanthera longiflora* and other poisonous plants. East Africa has been an important world source of ivory since Roman times, and it was as ivory poachers that the Wata achieved notoriety. In the early 1970s, the Lamu hinterland contained over 21,000 elephants, the largest single elephant population in the country. A decade later only a few thousand elephants remain. Although the Wata and Boni were certainly involved, it is the Somali Shifta, armed with modern automatic weapons, who are principally to blame for the decimation.

The Dahalo live close to and just south of the Boni around Witu, Kipini and Mkunumbi. They seemingly adopted and retained the Southern Cushitic language as their own, without becoming totally acculturated to the food-producer Cushites who were familiar with stock-raising and grain cultivation. The tsetse-ridden doum-palm-wooded grassland with its shallow swamps, often vivid with water lilies after the rains, that make up Dahalo territory was probably unsuited to pastoralism. Throughout the present millennium, and perhaps even earlier, the Dahalo maintained trading contacts with the agriculturalists and urban centres of the immediate coastal area. Much as the Boni and Wata in more recent times, the Dahalo bartered the results of their hunting activities and crafts (ivory, honey and carved woodwork, such as plates, bowls, walking sticks, combs and honey barrels).

The Yaaku, numbering perhaps 250 people, claim to be the original inhabitants of the Mukogodo area of Laikipia just north of Nanyuki, and at an earlier date may have occupied a much larger territory up to and around Lake Turkana. A hunter-gatherer group, they have turned to pastoralism in recent years – adopting many of the economic characteristics and culture of the Maasai, including the language. They were once one of several hunter-gatherer groups (the others being Okiek sections, the Digiri, Ilwaso, Mumonyot and, from the Meru side of Mount Kenya, the Ng'wesi) inhabiting the Mukogodo forests and trading arrow poisons, bee-hives and honey with the Samburu and, with the Somali, ivory and rhino horns. With the acquisition of stock they moved from the hillside caves they occupied in the forest to Maasai-style *manyatta* on the plains below, small family groups now dependent on a cattle-economy. Even today very little is known of their earlier lifestyle and research into their original Eastern Cushitic language continues.

Above: Deftly balancing a calabash on her head, a you *Boni bride returns home after drawing water from a nearby water-hole.*

Boran

EASTERN CUSHITIC

A section of the Oromo-speaking peoples of Southern Ethiopia, the Boran (69,000) moved south at the turn of the century into the arid areas of northeast Kenya to settle around Moyale, Marsabit and, even further south, along the Ewaso Ngiro river and in the Isiolo District.

The Oromo had erupted into the Christian Kingdom of Ethiopia in the sixteenth century, conquering and settling large parts of the country. But, between 1890 and 1900, the vast territories of the Oromo were subdued by Emperor Menelik II, and his policy of ruthless extermination and rapacious demands for tribute forced the Boran and other Ethiopian peoples (notably the Burji) to migrate into Kenya.

Predominantly cattle holders, although camels, sheep and goats are kept, the Boran believe in a supreme deity, *Wak*, with whom they communicate through a ritual expert or priest, the *Qallu*, and with sacrifices and prayer (*wadaja*). (The southernmost Boran, however, have been converted to the Muslim faith.) Living *Qallu* are regarded as the embodiment of the first: he was discovered as a full-grown man herding three black cows and a ram by a hunter-gatherer people, the Wata (sometimes Warta). Despised though they are, for no Boran would take a Wata for his wife or give his daughter to one, the Wata, who still roam the ridge of mountains to the west of Moyale, play an important role in Boran rituals. The *Qallu* continue to maintain herds of all-black cows, the descendants of those found with the first *Qallu*. These ritual leaders live in large Boran-style, flat-topped houses (*galma*) of grass laid over a framework of bent branches, situated deep in Ethiopia. Snakes are kept in bamboo containers in emulation of the original *Qallu*. A metal armlet (*ladu*) signifies the transfer of powers from the dead *Qallu* to his successor.

The Gona moiety, divided into the Ful'leli (Oditu, Dacitu, Gallantu, Konitu, Macitu, Bacitu and Sirraiyu) and Haroresa (Arussi, Hawartu, Qarcabdu, Jilitu, Nonitu and Dambitu) sub-sections, together with the Sabho (Digalu, Matari and Karaiyu) make up the Boran people. It is said the Gona kill no snakes except the puff adder, the Sabho all snakes but the puff adder.

A series of complex rituals and festivals marks the birth and naming of a Boran child. The first ceremony is more usually confined to relatives and close friends, whereas the whole community participates in the *jilla* ceremony – to name a child, to thank and seek the blessing of *Wak*. A large *galma*, modelled on that of the *Qallu*, is built in which a Wata, using firesticks, kindles the first fire. If the child is a boy, his head-tuft (*gutu*) is shaved off by his father who, after further feasting and singing, names the child. The following dawn a bullock is blessed and sacrificed. Narrow skin bracelets are cut from its hide for the child and relatives; a diviner reads the fortune of the boy and the meat is divided – the Wata, in gratitude for their discovery of the first *Qallu*, receive a share, together with gifts of milk. An auspicious day during or just after the rains, when milk is plentiful is selected for *jilla*, and a child may be between one to three years at the time of the festival. A girl child goes through a simpler *jilla* ceremony.

Before a young man is again allowed to grow a *gutu*, he has to establish his manhood by killing a man of another tribe, a lion or an elephant, or prove his virility as a father of a homestead (*aba worra*) by marrying and begetting a child. In the final year of the *gadamoji* cycle this *gutu* is plaited into the halo-like *guduru* to which is added the metal or ivory *kalacha*. There is a *gadamoji* ceremony every eight years. Each candidate in turn boasts of his prowess in individual battle, in hunting and in begetting children and makes a series of sacrifices – a bull on *barati* day at the start of the ceremony, a sheep on *elejesa* day and another bull on *buffat* day, when his elaborate *guduru* hair-do is ritually shaved by his wife and buried in the cattle-dung *dobu*. After a Boran has completed decorating his head and undergone the *gadamoji* ceremony and shaved off his *guduru* he should never again carry a spear, use abusive language or become involved in

Above: Women's necklaces and bracelets of gleaming aluminium testify to the skills of the Boran smith who fashioned them by melting down old pots known as sufuria.

Opposite: Colourfully dressed Boran woman intent on final touches to a new ceremonial dress of leather strap Decorated with beads and cowries, it is worn only to commemorate births or marriages or during her people two great ceremonies, jilla *and* gadamoji.

Below: Dawn infuses the harsh scrubland as members of a Boran household milk their emaciated cattle. Wooden containers are used for milking and wooden bowls and platters as household utensils.

Bottom: A Boran elder and father of the homestead (a worra), wearing the everyday turban, baddo, *made from a cloth called* kenso. *On ceremonial occasions the type of turban known as the* surri ruga *found with the infant* Qallu *is worn.*

an affray (unless under the most extreme provocation). He is respected and honoured.

The Boran are divided into five generation-sets (*luba*), each of which has its 'father' (*aba gada*) nominated by the elders, and takes the name of the appointed *aba gada* as its own. Four initiation cycles, each of eight years, separate the generations; forty years thus elapse between the initiation of father and son, who consequently belong to the same *luba*.

Payment of the bride wealth for a Boran girl, who may be circumcised at any time and without ceremony, is made in cattle, tobacco or dried coffee berries (*buni*). A Boran woman is confined to the *galma* for three weeks following the birth of a child, and may not drink milk, but is fed a diet of meat, soup and blood.

International and district boundaries and tribal grazing restrictions increasingly curtail the movement of the Boran, who congregate around the limited water points during the dry seasons and disperse to better grazing areas after the rains. Boran dislike wage labour and, in face of opposition from the elders, few migrate to the towns. Skilled stockmen, they are to be found on farms and ranches in many parts of Kenya. Despite educational advances and irrigation schemes along the Ewaso Ngiro, the Boran traditional lifestyle has so far been little disrupted.

Burji

EASTERN CUSHITIC

A settled agricultural people who formerly lived on the slopes of Gara Burji mountain, south-east of Lake Abaya in Southern Ethiopia, the Amaro-Burji were one of several Oromo-speaking peoples dislocated by the expansionist schemes of Emperor Menelik II. Many fled across the border into northern Kenya in the first decades of this century. By the end of his reign (1889–1913), the Emperor had more than doubled the original size of his empire, subdued the vast territories of the Oromo to the south and reduced the once proud Burji to virtual serfdom (*gabbar*). The Tigre uprising of 1916 which spread south from Northern Ethiopia exacerbated the tragic situation.

The first Burji man to seek refuge in Kenya was perhaps Hille Ume in about 1906. If so, he was the vanguard for several thousands of his people who settled in Moyale and later Marsabit, where the hilly, well-forested and fertile land was to the liking of the thrifty, agricultural Burji. There is now a small community of Burji traders in Nairobi.

In their former home the Burji cultivated maize, *teff*, beans, pumpkins, coffee, cotton, tobacco and bananas on the terraced hillsides of Gara Burji. The Burji claim never to have worn skins, and wove fine garments, *bado* and *kuta*, from the cotton they grew. A *bado* was sufficient for a girl's dowry. When the Burji crossed into Kenya, they left their goods and possessions behind. Now a dying craft, it was once common to see the old men and women seated under the eaves of their distinctive flat-roofed huts in Moyale spinning the cotton on to spindles. Later it would be woven into cloth on wooden looms.

Traditionally the tribal leadership is vested in the *Ganna*, a hereditary spiritual and political head. On his death, the succession passes to his son. In a ceremony marked by ritual and mystery, the ring of authority (*maldacho*) is transferred to his son, and the *Ganna* is then buried with his ivory adornments. The new *Ganna* is expected to marry a suitable girl of high status who becomes the queen (*Wonawa*). The first-born of this union, irrespective of any earlier marriages, becomes the heir.

The Amaro-Burji are divided into two major groups, the Burji and the Gubba. Each of the nine Burji clans (Qarado, Yabbi, Karama, Gamayo, Annabura, Umma, Goda, Woteish and Tamei) and the seven clans of the Gubba (Gashara, Otomali, Wordei, Rallel, Wallei, Yoban and Ladisle) has a spiritual and political head, *Gosang Ana*. Before the annual rains, the clan assembles at the homestead of the *Gosang Ana* who, in ceremonial garb, the *kalacha* sign on his forehead, a black cloth or *rufa* draped around his shoulders and a feather *balguda* in his hair, offers communal prayers and sacrifices a bull or goat to invoke rain, peace and prosperity.

Boys are circumcised between the ages of ten and fifteen, and after several groups have gone through the ceremony the age-group cycle is completed and they form one age-grade or *haga* and choose four members to represent them in the councils of the tribe. The eight age-grades of the Burji rotate, and are called Harbora, Qumbe, Yato, Mote, Barbara, Citawa, Kalala and Balla.

A girl's upbringing determines her eligibility for marriage. Girls are strictly watched by their mothers and aunts, and they are not allowed to fetch firewood or water or engage in other household chores which take them away from the homestead unless accompanied by a relative or female chaperon. For a girl to remain unmarried well past the usual age arouses comment and is a severe embarrassment to a respected family. The social status, caste and reputation of the girl are all taken into account by a young man contemplating marriage. When a man has made his choice of a wife, his mother and another elderly woman approach the girl's parents for formal discussions. Once agreement has been reached the wedding date is fixed, usually during the harvest period. Before the wedding day, the young people are forbidden to see each other, but once the girl's parents have signified their consent the 'marriage' takes place by

Above: Her strong arm swiftly whirling the traditional grindstones, a Burji woman prepares the family meal under the eaves of her Moyale home.

Opposite: Teff straw and cotton cloth form contrasts of gold and silver as a white-haired Burji demonstrates th. traditional art of weaving on his wooden hand-loom. In the past, lengths of this cloth made up the bado *and* kuta *garments essential for a girl's dowry.*

Below: Yoked oxen haul a single-furrow traditional plough through an arid Burji field. Despite their harsh environment the Burji are resourceful smallholders and the multi-purpose oxen are also used to tread out the grain after harvest or as pack animals.

Opposite: Using the time-honoured method, a Burji mother grinds out millet flour in front of her flat-toppe ochre-plastered house in a Moyale street.

elopement – friends of the young man assisting to carry off the girl. On the birth of the first child the husband presents the girl's parents with *darbata* (cloth).

A law-abiding community, the Burji became the principal agricultural labour force, and built roads and houses in the Moyale and Marsabit districts, within a few years of their crossing into Kenya. The greater number of Amaro-Burji remain in Gara Burji or scattered elsewhere in Southern Ethiopia. A number of Konso people, near-neighbours of the Burji in Ethiopia, have also crossed the border and settled in Moyale and Marsabit, although recent immigrants face deportation by the Administration.

Dassanich
EASTERN CUSHITIC

Only a few thousand Dassanich are permanently settled in Kenya, in the Todenyang area of Turkana and around Ileret, in Marsabit District at the northern tip of Lake Turkana, difficult of access and one of Africa's remote backwaters. Across the border in the Gamu Gofa Province of Ethiopia, where the main section are domiciled, perhaps as many as 20,000 Dassanich herd their stock and cultivate the Omo delta area and both banks of the river Omo as far as sixty kilometres upstream. Now a homogenous people divided into eight sections, the Dassanich are a relatively recent grouping of many disparate origins; offshoots of other Cushitic and Nilotic groups who have found common cause in adversity.

By the Turkana they are known also as the Merille. Oromo speakers call them the Gelubba, and early Austrian explorers Count Teleki and von Hohnel used the (probable) Samburu terminology for them, Reshiat. But it is as the Shankilla (their Amharic name) that cadres of young Dassanich, in alliance with the Ethiopian Hamer Koke, strike terror into the encampments of the Turkana, Gabbra and Rendille as they maraud and pillage deep into Kenyan territory.

The imperialistic ambitions of Emperor Menelik II and the occupation of the Omo region by his troops in 1898, together with British opposition to ivory and slave trading, left Turkanaland in turmoil. The Anglo–Ethiopian treaty of 1906, and that with Sudan in 1920, finally helped to stabilise the area. In 1937, however, the Italian conquest of Abyssinia once again made it possible for the Dassanich to acquire rifles (provided by the Italians up to 1941, just before they were driven out by the British) and despite the efforts of all authorities they have continued to harry their neighbours using their training in guerilla warfare.

Rains in the Ethiopian Highlands during October and November swell the Omo river, which floods down to inundate the delta area where it courses through several channels into Lake Turkana. During these months precipitated silt stains the jade waters of the lake brown for tens of kilometres to the south. As the floods recede the Dassanich plant and cultivate the river banks for a five- or six-month period; the traditional crops of sorghum, millet, beans and tobacco are augmented today with maize, vegetables and fruit. The long rains (March to May) are followed by the dry season, when the men move their livestock farther west in search of pasture. Large herds of cattle are kept, for cattle are central to social relationships and for ceremonial purposes. The dry season is the time of ritual sacrifice and feasting, of the annual *dimi* ceremonies which help to maintain an ecological balance and reduce the stock to numbers the land can carry. The Kenya Dassanich are not well endowed with livestock and fish the waters of Lake Turkana using harpoons, nets and basket traps. Often they travel in their dugout canoes down the east shore of the lake as far as Alia Bay or beyond, sun-drying their catch.

A man's generation-set (*hari*) is determined at his birth, for he automatically joins the alternate set to that of his father. His life-cycle is measured by a sequence of ceremonies which approximately parallel those of the life-cycle of a woman. Each son at birth receives a cow and a few female small stock. At the age of seven or eight, the first-born daughter receives the blessing of the elders (*ara* or 'bulls') in the elaborate *dimi* ceremony to ensure her own fertility and that of her sisters. The ritual slaughter of virtually his entire herd often leaves the father impoverished but enhanced in the status and prestige of eldership. On reaching puberty a boy passes through a ceremony (*uru*) which is symbolic of clitoridectomy. Transition from youth (*nigen*) to adulthood (*kabana*) is signified by the *me tagniya* ceremony, when small cliques of young men in their late teens change their hairstyles and obtain enhanced responsibilities and freedom to cooperate in raiding. Dassanich men are circumcised late and are often in their twenties or early thirties before they marry, establish their own households and

Above: A young Dassanich girl about to carry home a flask of water. Daughters are much cherished – and the dimi *ceremony with its elaborate ritual blessing of a girl and her sisters may impoverish the father while enhancing his status within the community.*

Opposite: Goats load down the dug-out canoe of a Dassanich pastoralist as he poles his craft ashore after crossing the 400-metre-wide Omo river of southern Ethiopia. The community live on both sides, ferrying their livestock across whenever grazing patterns alter. Small stock are a tempting snack for the crocodiles which abound in the Omo river, the main feeder for Kenya's Lake Turkana.

Above: A Dassanich herdsman and his son rest in their arid landscape, close to Kenya's northern border with Ethiopia. In such burnt-out wastelands cattle trek long distances for forage and water.

separate their personal livestock from those of their kinsmen.

Although the immediate economic benefits may be slight, for captured livestock and young girls are gifted to near relatives and friends and not retained by the raiders, on attaining *kabana* groups of young men engage in raids against neighbouring tribes. It is when banded with the Hamer Koke that marauding Ethiopian Dassanich penetrate deep into Kenyan territory. Killings effected in a mood of total aggression (*sariti*) are often cruel and deliberate. The Turkana, Gabbra and Rendille bear the brunt of these attacks and retaliation may result in periods of outright confrontation leading to the abandonment of villages and grazing grounds.

The Dassanich have a special bond with those who witness and take part in a successful raid in which enemy tribesmen are killed. The return of the raiders to their own village is greeted by dancing and singing and the young girls decorate them with necklaces. The killing of an enemy is followed by a series of cleansing rites; a white sheep (*ai chilan*) is slaughtered, the warrior's head is shaved and his generation-set share in the feast of the ox of the enemy (*ain kisiet*). The killer takes an honorary name (*yer nit kisiet*) and the scars (*chade*) that indicate his prowess are incised on his chest.

On the Ethiopian side of the border appropriate small-community technology introduced by American missionaries found a ready acceptance. But the missionaries were forced out following the death of Emperor Haile Selassie. The sails of the Cretan windmills no longer turn, for the Cuban agricultural advisers who now assist the Ethiopian administration have failed to sustain the impetus of development. In Kenya, more effective policing is containing the Shankilla raids. Enlarged marketing outlets have been provided for Dassanich fishermen to sell their entire catch to the newly opened Norwegian-financed refrigerated fish factory at Kalakol. Reluctantly but inevitably the Dassanich are accepting integration into the economic and political systems of Kenya.

El-Molo
EASTERN CUSHITIC

The el-Molo (numbering less than 500 people) live on two small islands and at Loiyangalani in the south-eastern corner of Lake Turkana (formerly Rudolf) in northern Kenya, an inhospitable region of wind-lashed lava and sun-scorched desert scrub. Only a few stunted acacias along the dried-up watercourses and clusters of doum palms relieve the desolation. The el-Molo subsist by fishing.

The history of the el-Molo is obscure. The name derives from the word *molo* meaning 'man', to which the Maasai-Samburu plural prefix *il* was added and anglicised as el-Molo. The el-Molo, who call themselves Ldes, are divided into four clans, the Lmarle, Orikara (Amkara), Origijijo and Ndes. The el-Molo are neither, as they are often depicted, 'Africa's smallest tribe' nor a 'dying race'; for even in Kenya the Yaaku and other hunter-gatherer peoples may be numerically smaller than the el-Molo who, through intermarriage with neighbouring Samburu and Turkana, have pulled themselves back from the threshold of extinction.

The el-Molo claim to have travelled to their present home in el-Molo Bay from the northern tip of Lake Turkana, perhaps from the Omo delta. The oral traditions of the el-Molo people detail not only how they came to start their 250-kilometre journey south, but also catalogue the promontories and sand-spits at which they stopped, perhaps for decades at a time, en route. Legend has it that long ago the el-Molo lived far to the north. One day the men left to go fishing some distance from their village. While they were away raiders from the interior attacked the defenceless village, spearing to death the unprotected women and children who had been left behind. When the men returned, they found their families slaughtered and their belongings and livestock looted. Saddened by the killing, and fearful that the raiders might return, they decided to leave that place of sorrow. Together with a few survivors of the massacre they set out south, eventually reaching el-Molo Bay.

The majority of el-Molo now speak Samburu. Only a few elders still speak the tribe's indigenous language (closely related to and possibly an earlier dialect of Rendille). Shared cultural traits such as the burying of their dead in stone cairns and belief in a deity called *Wak* suggest that the el-Molo may derive from an earlier group of neighbouring Rendille pastoralists turned permanent fishermen.

Fresh or dried fish form the staple food of the el-Molo, augmented by crocodile, turtle and hippopotamus meat. Wild game and birds are also eaten. The el-Molo account for their former lack of domestic animals with the tale that long ago they, too, owned stock. Their animals, however, were not camels, cattle, sheep and goats but hippopotamuses, crocodiles and turtles. Each morning these would be driven to feed on the grass and aquatic weeds along the lake shore, returning in the evening. Like camels and cattle, they were milked and bled for food. One day, while the men were away fishing, a careless el-Molo woman who was drawing water had her pot blown into the lake by a sudden gust of wind. Seeing the pot floating away, she called to the hippopotamuses, crocodiles and turtles to help recover it before it was irretrievably lost. The animals quickly entered the water and swam after the pot, now bobbing along on the waves far offshore. Soon, like the pot, they had disappeared beyond the horizon. From that day to this, the animals have never returned to dry land, and that, say the el-Molo, is why they are a people who live only by fishing.

The el-Molo construct doum palm rafts with which to fish and communicate with el-Molo Island. Three to six logs (*ilkadishi*) are loosely tied together with fibre ropes made from the leaves of the doum palm. Part of the bride wealth payment traditionally consisted of two such fishing rafts. When dry, these el-Molo rafts are capable of transporting three to four adults (larger rafts incorporating perhaps a dozen logs are used to move whole families and their belongings) but the fibrous wood of the doum palm quickly becomes

Opposite: Silhouetted against the sinking sun, el-Molo youngsters punt home their doum-palm log raft with the day's scavenging of browse for the island's goats.

Below: The el-Molo inhabitants of two small islands off the south-east shore of Lake Turkana pose for a clan portrait. The women are wearing traditional doum palm fibre aprons. More recently, the el-Molo have abandoned their island homesteads for the mainland amenities of Loiyangalani.

waterlogged, limiting the use of the rafts to no more than a few hours at a time. A long pole is used to punt the raft along in the shallow waters around the islands or the lake shore. In the deeper water the pole (*yoo*, pl. *yooni*) is used horizontally, much like an Eskimo kayak paddle.

The el-Molo employ three traditional methods of fishing; harpooning, netting and hook and line. In recent years, the Turkana basket fish-trap has also been adopted. Harpoons are constructed by inserting a barbed metal head, to which a long fibre rope is secured, into one end of a wooden shaft so that it can be jabbed or thrown to catch the giant Nile perch. Against crocodile or hippopotamus, ordinary throwing spears are also used to ensure a kill. Fishing nets are woven from twisted, doum palm-fibre string to catch tilapia, other small fish and turtles. Barbless-hook and line fishing is practised in shallow water from the shore.

Personal ornaments are not as elaborate as those of the neighbouring Samburu and Turkana. The women wear multiple strings of ostrich-egg or glass beads. Wrist and elbow bracelets of metal are worn by both men and women. Distinctive, bowl-shaped pottery vessels once made from clay dug from pits on the island have been replaced today by cheap aluminium cooking pots (*sufuria*). The dome-shaped, circular el-Molo huts are built of interlaced acacia branches and covered with doum palm leaves, reeds, grass or other vegetation held against the torrid winds by stones. Woven palm-leaf mats are used for sleeping.

The el-Molo today are changing rapidly. New fishing techniques are being introduced and at Loiyangalani they are turning to cattle keeping and wage employment at the nearby lodge, or fishing commercially to supplement their traditional form of subsistence in larger, more permanent and better housed settlements.

low: Dexterity with the harpoon is mastered early by
Molo youngsters steeped in the fishing traditions of
eir ancestors. Fishing is a means of survival, a daily
ore for all members of the family.

Below: El-Molo hippo hunters butcher a carcass.
Throughout, the hunters drone a dirge of triumph as the
meat is cut into thin strips and sun-dried before the trek
home. In the village women and girls will dance and sing
the praises of the hunter who threw the first harpoon.
To him, by tradition, go the prized trophies, ears, tail
and tongue.

low: An el-Molo hunter wades waist deep in Lake
rkana's jade waters in pursuit of a crocodile.

ttom: A Nile crocodile snaps in torment and
istration as his el-Molo captors hold taut their roped
rpoons. The final despatch, by severing the spinal cord
th spear jabs, is often desperate and dangerous for the
Molo hunters.

Below: The slain crocodile is dragged into the shallows
where the prime cuts – tail and other selected portions –
are quickly removed from the carcass.

posite: Immature crocodiles near an el-Molo village expect short shrift from their own age-group. Four
Molo youngsters triumphantly carry home the
phy that vindicates their prowess.

Below: In the village, the butchering of the young
crocodile is supervised by two senior members of the
community.

Embu

CENTRAL BANTU

The Embu (180,500) occupy a 512 square kilometre district of the same name in Eastern Province on the south-eastern slopes of Mount Kenya. It is a country of many fast-flowing streams dropping swiftly into the Tana river, which drains into the Indian Ocean. The Embu people represent the assimilation of successive waves of immigrants from Meru to the north-east, Kikuyu to the west and Mbeere to the south, into one indigenous society. The belief is strengthened by tradition, for it is said that the Embu are descendants of a man called Mwenendega who kidnapped his wife, Nthara, when she was bathing in a stream near Runyenje's market. Their children, a boy called Kembu and a girl named Werimba, were chased from their parents' home when the girl was made pregnant by her brother. They, their children, and additional sons and daughters of Mwenendega and Nthara, settled the Embu district.

Alternatively, it is claimed that the Embu people came from 'beyond Meru', perhaps in a time of famine, and crossed the Thuchi river near Ishiara where they split, the Mbeere taking a southerly route. The elders say the Embu fought and drove out the hunter-gatherer Gumba with the aid of hornbills who cried like Embu warriors to frighten the Gumba. At first, it is said, they lived in forest caves before moving into the open country they inhabit today.

The Embu descend from two main moieties or divisions: the Ngua (or Thagana) and the Gavati (or Irumbi), which in turn are divided into some twenty-six clans. The Ngua clans are the Kithami, Gicuku, Igambua, Ngai (Ngandori), Rwamba, Bandi, Kathuci, Igamukira, Riimi, Njuki, Muthiga, Ngithi and Muthanga. The Gatavi clan names are Mariigu, Ngiiri, Kina, Rukwaru, Gitiri, Gikiri, Ngai (Kieni), Igamuturi, Ndiri, Igandu, Thara, Ndangi and Magwi.

Although nowadays hunting and gathering contribute little to the economy, the Embu are notable bee-keepers and during the late nineteenth century hunted elephant for ivory with weighted spear-traps and pits. This they exchanged for cloth, metal and beads with the Arab-Swahili caravans from the coast which traded through the area. With a well-distributed rainfall, the rich, fertile chocolate coloured loams support a variety of crops. The traditional arrowroot, yams, bananas, sweet potatoes, cassava, several kinds of peas and beans and maize have been joined by cotton, coffee, tea and pyrethrum; these valuable cash crops are marketed through cooperative societies. Cattle, sheep and goats are kept.

The Embu were skilled in a number of crafts. The traditional blacksmith's workshop (*kiganda*, pl. *iganda*), as among so many of Kenya's peoples, was a place of awe; here were made spears, axes, arrow-heads and swords (*simi*) as well as ear-rings, leg-bells and other small items. The iron ore used was either alluvial or came from old articles re-smelted. Basket work, especially large trays (*gitaruru*, pl. *itaruru*) and wicker-work shields, the making of calabash dishes and gourds – often decorated with shells – and the carving of stools and wooden dishes and leatherwork are dying crafts today, but formerly of great importance in the Embu economy.

Circumcision marks the point at which a boy (*kivici*) becomes a warrior (*mwanake*). The whole neighbourhood celebrates a circumcision (*mwana ti wa mundu umwe*: a child does not belong to one person alone). No Embu girl should traditionally reach her menarche before clitoridectomy; and marriage quickly follows. Circumcision is but one of a number of life-cycle ceremonies (*maambura*). As a young Embu *mwanake* demonstrates his abilities as a warrior and moves into elderhood he is expected to pay to his seniors a succession of goats – until he, in turn, achieves a seat on the war council (*njama ya ita*) and among the senior elders (*kiama kia ngome*).

The traditional Embu homestead usually constitutes a small patrilineal family group, linking two or three generations. The head of the family has his

Opposite: Embu banana seller in colourful Ishiara market, main trade and meeting centre for the Embu, Mbeere and Tharaka people.

own hut, close to the opening in the *miururi* hedges that enclose the homestead – with the huts of his wives (for polygamy was, and in many cases still is, the ideal) around the perimeter of the enclosure. The younger children and unmarried girls live in their mother's hut. The traditional circular Embu mud and wattle hut with its conical thatch roof has generally been replaced with modern, often stone-built homes of rectangular construction with corrugated, galvanised sheeting roofs.

Subsistence farming has given way to cash crops on consolidated holdings following demarcation and the granting of individual title deeds, and the Embu are swiftly proving themselves one of Kenya's most progressive agricultural peoples.

Opposite: Ripening cherries on a well-manicured coffee farm at Karurumo, Embu District, on the slopes of Mount Kenya.

Left: Fondness for music and dance inspires an Embu flute player to demonstrate traditional skills at a day of national celebrations.

Opposite: Withies of a local shrub form the framework of a chicken coop when woven by skilled Embu craftsman.

Gabbra
EASTERN CUSHITIC

The Gabbra of Marsabit District in Eastern Province are mainly a camel-owning people, although many thousands of hardy Boran cattle and flocks of goats and fat-tailed sheep are kept. Except for a small section occupied by the Dassanich at the tip of Lake Turkana, the Gabbra graze their livestock over the whole area east of the lake, a tract of northern Kenya which includes the Chalbi Desert, the Huri Hills and the Dida Galgallu plains stretching up to the border with Ethiopia.

One of the Oromo-speaking peoples forced south-west out of Southern Ethiopia by the depredations of Emperor Menelik's troops, the Gabbra are subject to continuous Somali pressure for control of grazing and water along their eastern boundary; a manifestation, together with the Shifta war of the mid-1960s and the more recent Somali adventure into the Ogaden region of Ethiopia, of the on-going attempt to implement the political concept of a Greater Somalia. Virtually all Gabbra, numbering 30,500, are now domiciled in Kenya.

The Gabbra make their encampment with fibre mats and skins laid over a dome-shaped frame of withies lashed together. A homestead consists of a man, his wives and married children. A village may encompass anything from two to twenty homesteads. In the Huri Hills, where there is excellent grazing but no permanent water, the cattle villages of the Gabbra converge for a month or two if the rains are good. Then, when the water pans are dry, they disperse again to the wells in the plains.

In the desert, milking camels require water only every five or six days, dry camels at more infrequent intervals. Long caravans of Gabbra camels, herded by the young women of the tribe, are brought in to Marsabit from up to eighty kilometres away to water at the mountain springs and wells. The fibre water-containers of the homesteads are filled and lashed on to the camels for the return journey, two or more days' march.

Considered 'junior' to the Boran proper, the Gabbra have no *Qallu* (ritual expert) of their own and are divided not into moieties but into clans, three large and three small. The Algana, a large clan, and the Dolio, a minor one, are linked with the Sabho moiety of the Boran. The Gara and the Galbo, both major clans, and the Odolla and the Sarbana are linked with the Gona. Unlike the Sakuye, few Gabbra have accepted the Islamic faith and although the Roman Catholic Church has missions at North Horr, Sololo and Maikona the Gabbra retain a strong commitment to their traditional religious beliefs.

The seniority of the Boran among the Oromo-speaking peoples is further reflected in their possession of generation-sets not shared with the Gabbra, Sakuye and Wata. The Gabbra have generation-sets of their own, similar but having no relationship to those of the Boran. The Sakuye do not possess such sets. A generation-set (*luba*) is a group of circumcised men of the same section who, having assumed their social responsibilities and status in a transitional feast called *jilea* (sometimes *jilea galana*), proceed together and gradually assume higher social status and responsibilities in successive *jilea*. The Gabbra generation-sets are named Wagura, Wakor, Gurjab, Afata, Manguba and Damela. A man initiated into a generation-set belongs to it throughout his lifetime, although he and his colleagues in the same set enter new grades and take on enhanced responsibilities. The people of the Galbo clan recognise four such grades, Komicha, Yuba, Dabela and Jarsa. The Komicha are young men who gradually take over full responsibility for ruling the tribe. Yuba are those who steadily relinquish responsibility until they become Dabela, who have the task of enacting ritual and religious ceremonies. Eventually they retire to become Jarsa, old men. Sons take their status at a *luba* separated by one intermediate *luba* from that of their fathers. Married women belong to that of their husbands. Children and unmarried girls have no *luba*. The seven-year *luba* cycle is too short to give a man the opportunity to fulfil his functions within his

Above: Desert sun and hardship have weathered deep lines of experience in this Gabbra elder's face. He is one of a select group of leaders, jallaba, *who adjudicate disputes over water and grazing.*

Opposite: Leather vessels are used to scoop the muddy water into sun-baked troughs by Gabbra herdsmen watering their camels near Sololo. Gabbra territory east of Lake Turkana is lava-strewn and barren of all but a few acacias and poor grasslands.

grade and for this reason the transition feasts (*jilea*) are often postponed and may take place at intervals of twenty years or more.

The careful reckoning of time is essential to the Gabbra, not only for practical everyday uses but also for their rituals, in particular the great socio-religious *jilea*. Seven *ayana* or days (*ad*, *alsinina*, *talassa*, *arba*, *kamisi*, *gumota*, *sabdi*) make up the Gabbra week (*torban*), although the days are also called other names after some animals. The names of the weekdays are also the names of successive years (*ganna*). Every seven years a new 'set' of years patterned on the week-cycle commences. A year is the period of time extending between consecutive feasts of the *Almado*, 365 days divided into various sections. The Gabbra count 100 days immediately after *Almado*. This is the season of hot weather and frequently a time of drought. The second 100 days is the period of the long rains. This is followed by sixty-six days corresponding to the cool but dry weather following the rains; then a spell of fourteen days during which the Odolla clan light the ritual fires; and finally, a ten-week period (paradoxically named the 'nine weeks', *torban sagal*) which culminates in the fifteen-day period of *Almado* during which three feasts are celebrated to signal the end of one year and the beginning of another.

The customs, utensils and ornaments of the Gabbra are characteristic of the Oromo-speaking people. One attractive and distinctive Gabbra ornament, however, is the double band of aluminium beads worn by Gabbra women around their heads. These many-faceted beads are hand-fashioned from melted-down metal pots (*sufuria*); the hot metal is poured into channels in moist sand, then segmented into squares and the facets added by hammering the cold metal blanks to shape. Plaited fibre containers and wooden utensils are the usual household effects.

Marsabit Secondary School and the primary institutions at Maikona, North Horr and Sololo are preparing the younger members of the tribe for a more settled life, and although many Gabbra have moved to these minor townships the great majority of these handsome, thrifty people continue to traverse the vast semi-arid area to the west and north of Marsabit in pursuit of grazing for their stock – a way of life singularly unaffected by the restrictions of the twentieth century.

Gusii
WESTERN BANTU

The Gusii, Kenya's sixth largest tribal group (944,000), occupy the Kisii District and six locations of South Nyanza District (the other locations being Luo). Administered from Kisii, the Abagusii, as they refer to themselves, claim a common origin with the Kuria and Suba to the south and with the Luyia.

The traditions of the Gusii people indicate that they originated from a homeland far to the north termed *Misri* (Egypt), although it is unlikely that this dispersal area is synonymous with the modern state. From Mount Elgon the Gusii migrated southwards down the Nzoia river to the eastern shores of Lake Victoria. Turning east during the second half of the sixteenth century, they followed the lake shore, halting perhaps for several generations at a time. However, subjected to the pressure of successive waves of Luo immigration, they migrated steadily eastwards, stopping near Kisumu and in the Nyando valley before entering their present homeland in the Kisii highlands some two centuries ago.

Traditionally each of the numerous clans (*chiamate*) forms a semi-independent local community: the homestead head settles disputes and violations of authority and, as a final measure, is able to introduce the supernatural power of the curse on disobedient sons and daughters. Marked respect (*asoni*) is demanded between father and son, but this authority is not limitless. The clan elders sitting in council judge the more serious offences, for only they can perform the various sacrifices required to bring down divine retribution on the culprits and mete out punishment. The *Omogambi* is a senior elder charged with a socio-religious and political role, but not a 'chief' in the sense of those functionaries who were introduced by the British.

Surrounded as they were by the warlike Maasai and Kipsigis, the lack among the Gusii of political and military organisation at a higher level than the clan proved to be a weakness. For protection of their cattle, the Gusii formerly herded their stock at night into communal fortified enclosures (*ebisarate*) where a measure of protection was afforded them by the clan warriors. Cattle are immensely valued for bride wealth; between ten and twenty cattle are required to contract a marriage, and smaller stock are not acceptable substitutes. Cattle are needed for sacrifices and play a vital role in the economy of the Gusii. The blessing of the ancestral spirits is sought for 'increase of cattle and people'.

It took several punitive expeditions (notably in 1905 and 1908) before the British succeeded in bringing Gusiiland under control. The appointment of chiefs and headmen started at the end of 1907, but the Gusii people remained suspicious of British intentions and were slow to adopt the 'benefits' of Westernisation. Many Gusii rejected the imported, alien values and embraced the cult of Mumboism — a millennial movement which advocated the return to the lost glory and dignity of the tribe and belief in the old prophets. The cult was started in 1913 by a Luo, Onyango Dunde, who reported that he had been swallowed and then regurgitated by a huge snake. The reptile's instructions were carried into South Nyanza by Mosi, a headman from the Kabongo location. Mumboism, with its dreams and ecstatic ritual and belief in the imminent departure of the Europeans, remained a disruptive influence among the Gusii until it was banned in 1954.

Economically the Gusii cooperate to a much greater extent with the Luo than they do with their other neighbours, the Maasai and the Kipsigis. Trade links with the Luo are traditional. The Kisii highlands are fertile and extensively cultivated and abundant millet and maize have made them the granary of the Luo who live in the relatively drier lowlands. Gusii iron hoes and spears and soapstone dust (used for ceremonial decorative purposes) were other products bartered with the Luo for livestock, cattle-salt, fish, woven baskets and pots. Until fairly recently, the Gusii depended on traditional subsistence crops such as bananas, millet, eleusine and maize, but today the fertile Kisii highlands are one

Opposite: Verdant contrast to arid northern Kenya: a Gusii smallholding in the country's south-western highlands yields rich harvests of bananas, maize and vegetables. The thatched, conical roof of the farmhouse serves as protection against the torrential rains which ensure the Kisii highlands' year-round fertility.

Below: Safely cradled against her mother's back, a Gusii baby girl chortles with delight. The Gusii, with one of the world's highest birthrates, also have one of the highest population densities in Kenya, close to 700 people to the square kilometre.

of the prime tea, coffee and pyrethrum-producing areas of Kenya and passion fruit is a recently introduced exotic cash crop. More and more grade cattle are being kept on the well-planned smallholdings around the neatly thatched homesteads.

The white and delicately rose-hued soapstone, quarried locally in the Itumbe area, is now the basis of a major cottage industry employing many thousands of craftsmen, working in their own homes or in small cooperative workshops. The soft soapstone is easily sculpted with chisel and knife and the vast range of animal statuettes, candlesticks, vases and bric-à-brac is sold to handicraft shops in Nairobi and other major towns and tourist hotels along the Kenya coast. Master sculptor Elkana Ong'esa's greatest work now stands outside the Paris headquarters of UNESCO.

The Gusii are notable athletes, and Kenya's initial successes in international meetings came in the 1950s from such long distance runners as Nyandika Maiyoro and Arere Anentia. This tradition was upheld two decades later by Commonwealth and Olympic Games medallists Charles Asati (400 metres), Robert Ouko (800 metres) and Naftali Temu (5,000 and 10,000 metres).

Above: A yellow shawl worn with casual simplicity heightens the skin tone of a pretty Gusii country girl.

...ht and below: Sculpting Kisii soapstone has become ...basis of a handicrafts industry. Quarried out of the ...ing Kisii hillsides, the stone when fresh can be sawn ... timber into thin slabs from which platters, trays, ...ssboards and more intricate works of art can be ...ved. The Gusii have an older traditional use for their ...sitive hands – in delicate brain surgery.

Ilchamus
EASTERN NILOTIC

Closely related to the Samburu and Maasai, the Ilchamus of Lake Baringo number only 7,500. But unlike their cattle-herding relatives, the Maa-speaking Ilchamus (also Itiamus or Njemps from anglicisation of their original name, Il Chempus) are also agriculturalists, although they keep many cattle and large flocks of sheep and goats. The Ilchamus probably evolved as a political and cultural entity in the first half of the nineteenth century. Legend has it that the ol Doigio section of the Samburu, due to drought and loss of their stock, merged with the hunter-gatherer Il Geroi who were already resident around the lake.

A hundred years ago the Ilchamus used the waters of the Perkerra and Molo rivers to irrigate their traditional crops of millet and sorghum with which they supplied the caravans of Joseph Thomson and Count Teleki and other early European travellers. In lyrical prose, Thomson wrote of 'four small islets – a group of nature's emeralds in a dazzling setting of burnished silver'. Today's reality is very different. The 130 square kilometre lake has an average depth of under four metres. The waters are brown and muddy, and the islands barren rock. The arid Baringo area has been devastated by soil erosion and drought is perennial. When the rains fall in the Kabarnet hills, the impoverished topsoil, rocks and even trees are carried down the steep valleys by the deluge, with the result that Lake Baringo is silting up.

The Ilchamus have retained much of their Maasai heritage, although they have adopted the round huts of the neighbouring Kalenjin-speaking Tuken. Some seven major and five minor villages and two trading centres, the latter shared with several ethnic groups, make up the Njemps location of Baringo. The settlements in the west are said to be the oldest and those in the east more recent in time. Twelve intermarrying clans make up the patrilineal and somewhat conservative Ilchamus.

During the long droughts the Ilchamus graze their stock along the receding shoreline of the lake, and many augment their subsistence economy by fishing, using both nets and long lines of baited hooks. *Tilapia nilotica* is indigenous to the lake. The fishermen use canoe-shaped rafts made of ambatch stems bound together with sansevieria fibre rope. The ambatch (*Aeschynomene elaphroxylon*) grows in water to a height of four metres. Its bulbous, pithy stem is ten to twenty centimetres thick and, when dry, as light as cork. The rafts have a prow and open stern and are propelled by means of two scoop-shaped pieces of wood, about thirty centimetres in length, used as hand-paddles. Although utilised mainly for fishing, the rafts have an inner deck for greater rigidity and are used to transport livestock and passengers across the lake.

The Ilchamus practise both circumcision and clitoridectomy. It is considered a grave dishonour if a girl becomes pregnant before this rite has been performed. In such cases the operation is hastily carried out, and the seriousness of the crime is painfully impressed on the girl by the placing of ants (*ngalawo*) from the *tuwey* tree on the wound. Some two weeks in advance of actual circumcision (*muratare elaiyoni* if it refers to males; *muratare ndito* if clitoridectomy) and after part-payment of the bride wealth the bracelet (*il kiporket*) and white beads (*ngoriki il kiporket*) are worn by the girl who is to be initiated into womanhood. She sleeps on a special bed of *sokotei* tree leaves. On the morning of the actual excision she receives the blessing of the elders and is anointed by her female sponsors with butter, milk and ochre. After the operation she retires to rest while the special *saiyakia* circumcision dance is held. An Ilchamus girl is expected to marry immediately following clitoridectomy in her early teens, a practice which militates against the education of girls beyond the very first standards of primary school. Today, many Ilchamus men completing their higher education prefer to seek wives from the neighbouring, more sophisticated Tuken.

Two days before the bride is to marry and leave her home the groom and his

Opposite: Former pastoralists turned fishermen, Ilchamus unload their catch on the shores of silt-laden Lake Baringo in the heart of the Great Rift Valley.

entourage give three sheep to her senior female relatives for ritual slaughter and feasting. The next day there is the decorating of the bride, *il rikoret*. That evening the haggle over the terms of the payment of bride wealth (*mkukoo*), takes place. On the morning of the marriage the bride's eldest paternal and maternal uncles make ox-hide sandals (*yamata onamoka*) for her and she is dressed in black robes and her skin oiled with animal fat. Her ears and ear-rings and necklaces are ochred and as she leaves with her new in-laws on the walk to her husband's homestead she passes through two lines of elders who spit milk on her in blessing.

The young men (*layien*, pl. *layok*) of the tribe undergo a month's seclusion in the bush following circumcision, hunting birds (which they hang around their heads) with arrows blunted by balls of resin. For fun, they also shoot at small girls who, if hit, have to present them with a trophy, an iron link for their ankle ornaments. The lower two incisors are extracted, ear lobes are pierced to take the large ivory ear plugs (*sura*) and cicatrices are made on the stomachs of the youths. As warriors they will ochre their hair and dress it in elaborate styles and wear the toga-like cloth (*nanga*) in a fashionable drape around their bodies. Forehead and chin straps, bead chokers, bracelets and decorations mark the status of the warrior. His spears and other weapons are similar to those of the Maasai, but the finger-knife (*likardati*) and wrist-knife (*pade*) may be adopted from the neighbouring Pokot. Decoration of the elders is less elaborate, for their status is apparent from their copper ear-rings (*mintoni*) and a preoccupation with their snuff boxes (*ilkido*).

Dancing is an expression of personal art among the Ilchamus. The moving up of an age-grade, a circumcision, the birth of a baby, the onset of the rains or simply a spontaneous need are reason enough for dancing. *Ncha* is the everyday dance, *Sesie*, with its frankly sexual symbolism, a dance of men and women. *Inkindonberie* is danced by men, mainly the warrior group, to induce a sense of euphoria. *Ntiol* is another dance confined to the men. A fifth popular dance is *il kamase*. Women clap, pass comments (often ribald) and may dance in small groups on the fringe of the area. *Lolmune* (oxen game) is a women's dance.

Today, however, Lake Baringo is only a sixty-minute drive from Nakuru on a fast, all-weather road. Tourist lodges attract increasing numbers of visitors to the lake, which is renowned for its bird life, especially the nesting colony of Goliath herons and Verreaux's eagle. Inevitably, the traditional way of life of the Ilchamus is being affected by these contacts.

Above: Ilchamus fisherman wades home. Though shallow and laden with a silt of precious topsoil washed down from the Rift escarpments, Lake Baringo still yields a prolific harvest of wholesome tilapia fish.

Opposite: Like an ancient coracle of pre-history, an Ilchamus ambatch raft, a frail vessel made of sansevier fibre and a balsa-like wood which flourishes in the lake shallows, hauls in a night's catch on Baringo's placid waters.

Iteso
EASTERN NILOTIC

The Iteso of Busia and Bungoma districts of Western Province belong to the Ateker ('people of one language') family of tribes, which includes the Turkana in Kenya, the Iteso, Karamoja, Jie and Dodoth of Uganda and the Toposa, Jiye and Doniyiro of the Sudan. The original Iteso homeland was probably somewhere in the Sudan, from where they migrated to Karamoja in Uganda. Population pressures, famine and harassment by the Turkana and Karamoja forced them to disperse in the latter part of the seventeenth century. The Kenya Iteso (132,500) resulted from the drift eastwards between 1750 and 1850.

Permanent settlement by the warlike Iteso in the plains to the south of Mount Elgon brought them into conflict with the Luyia, especially the Bukusu. Endless Iteso raids laid waste vast stretches of country; and the Elgumi – as they were called by the Maasai – were reported by Joseph Thomson in 1883 as being greatly feared by the neighbouring Luyia. In 1890 the German explorer Dr Carl Peters received appeals from Luyia leaders Sakwa, Mumia and Dindi for military aid against the Iteso. Such raids resulted primarily from the Iteso desire to obtain cattle, but although mainly pastoralists they were also cultivators. Agriculture finally had a stabilising effect and the Iteso began to barter produce for small stock which in turn were exchanged for the cattle they coveted. Eleusine and millet, cow-peas, sim-sim, bananas, cassava, sweet potatoes and groundnuts were the indigenous crops grown to supplement their meat and milk diet. Iteso artisans had won renown as skilled potters even before their transmigration from Uganda across the border into Kenya. At Amukura today both men and women cooperate in the craft. The large, distinctive pots (amoti, pl. amotoi) are made from greyish clay found in the area. When eight or more pots have been prepared and thoroughly air-dried for some ten days to two weeks they are stacked together and covered with dry firewood and wet grass, to retain the heat and prevent the fire from burning too fiercely. Firing of the pots takes about one hour.

A major use of pots, apart from sale and the storage of grains and other household foods and the collection and storage of water, is in the manufacture of beer (ajono). Maize flour is fermented with water, pounded and left for some six days; the mixture is then fried and dried. Partially germinated millet (asipa) and water are added and after a further few days the brew is ready. Those invited to a drinking session sit around the pot, men on stools and women on mats, and sip the brew through long straws (epi, pl. ipiina). Beer drinking is the traditional reward for assisting in communal tasks, such as clearing land and building huts.

The Iteso live in homesteads scattered across the plains; the few main huts (etogo, pl. itogoi) are 'open plan' in form, with a place for the sheep and goats opposite the entrance. The huts are usually surrounded by a covered verandah (akadapan) which not only provides an outside area for the household chores but also, on occasion, for the playing of bau (elee). The board (atuba), with its rows of scooped out hollows and dried seeds, with which the game is played, is placed close to the doorway. Several stores (edula, pl. iduloi) surround the compound and since cattle raids are no longer common the cattle are tied to pegs close to the main hut.

The naming of a new-born baby is the responsibility of the paternal grandmother. After the baby has been secluded for the first week of its life, she and women age-mates within the clan visit the child. They bring with them a new calabash of millet beer into which the grandmother dips her finger and places it in the baby's mouth. She recites the names of relatives known for their prowess or good deeds. If the baby sucks strongly on her finger at the mention of a particular name, that is the one chosen. If the baby fails to respond, recourse is made to a magician – for perhaps two individuals seek to have the baby named after them? The magician places two hens (for a girl) or two cocks (for a boy) on

Opposite: Both pride and satisfaction are reflected in the face of an Iteso pot-maker of Amukura, near Busia, in western Kenya. Unsurpassed for craftsmanship and quality, Iteso-made pottery finds a ready market in nearby urban centres.

Below: A major function of Iteso pottery is to provide large urns for the community's tradition of social drinking. Filled with millet beer, the pot is placed in the centre of a group who draw beer through long straws, ipiina, made from hollow creepers. Bottom: The Iteso potter's art has been channelled by gifted exponents into works of sculpture. Fashioning fine clay figurines, this girl will fire the raw statuettes in the traditional manner and sell the finished work to curio shops.

Opposite top: An Iteso elder warms himself in the sun outside his grass-thatched traditional rondavel.

Opposite bottom: A young stockman tends a herd of small, long-horned Iteso cattle. Years ago, the Iteso were notorious cattle raiders, stealing stock from the neighbouring Bukusu and other tribes.

the thatched roof of the hut and each is named for one of the two possible choices. The first chicken to flutter from the roof resolves the issue.

The Iteso five-stringed harp (*adeudeu*) is a beautiful instrument. The base is formed of a resonant wooden bowl, oblong in shape and completely covered with hide. A hole is left in the membrane at the top of the bowl to release the sound. The stem of the instrument runs three-quarters of the way under the hide membrane and then extends outwards and upwards in a graceful curve. Wooden tuning pegs are fixed on the curve and the strings of twisted tendons are fastened at one end to that part of the stem which is under the membrane and stretched diagonally across the instrument to the tuning pegs. The Iteso are also skilled drummers, using the double-ended *atenesu* drum, which may be round or square in section. Ankle bells (*esifiria*) are an accompaniment to Iteso songs and dances. The *akolodong* and *adongo* are other Iteso musical instruments.

Nowadays the growing of maize, cotton, sugar cane and tobacco on a commercial basis and the consolidation of previously fragmented holdings have resulted in a departure from communal land ownership and the shifting agriculture practised in the past. Holdings are sizable, ranging from a few hectares to thirty hectares or more. Livestock improvement is a requirement, and the impetus of development throughout western Kenya is certain also to push the Iteso into more zealous farming activities. Coppices of gum trees (eucalyptus species) testify to the success of President Moi's call for afforestation to protect the environment, and the open plains of the Iteso are fast changing in character.

Kamba
CENTRAL BANTU

Occupying the Machakos and Kitui districts of Eastern Province, the Akamba are a people of the plains. Numbering 1,725,600 they are the fourth largest ethnic group in Kenya. The Athi river, becoming the Sabaki in its lower reaches, is the most important drainage system in the district. Distinctive features of the Ukambani area are the numerous granitic and volcanic hills, many of them exposed ridges of bare rock, rising a thousand metres or more above the plains. The Kamba account for their presence in the region with the myth that *Mulungu* (God, the Supreme Being) projected the first Kamba man and woman on to Mount Nzaui. There they were joined by another couple from the centre of the earth. *Mulungu* sent rain, and the land was made fertile and the Kamba people prospered.

Speculation still surrounds the origins of the Kamba, the probability being that they migrated to their present homeland from Kilimanjaro in the south. Alternatively, they may have branched off from the northward drift of coastal Bantu peoples or come from an ancient dispersal centre among the Mijikenda. Hunters, who also kept some livestock and cultivated millets and sorghums, the Kamba would appear to have become established four centuries ago at Mbooni, taking advantage of the higher rainfall and fertile soils to adopt a more sedentary life as agriculturalists. From Mbooni they eventually colonised the whole area.

Following early trade in arrow poisons and iron implements with the neighbouring Kikuyu, Embu, Tharaka and Mijikenda, a second stage in the growth of the Kamba economy commenced. By 1840, arrivals of Kamba caravans loaded with ivory were being reported almost weekly at the coast; in return they traded glass beads, copper, cotton fabrics, blue calico and salt for barter in the interior.

Masaku, diviner and medicine-man, commanded deep respect among his people; he prophesied the coming of the railway – 'the long snake' – and the Europeans who would divide the country. By this time Masaku's (corrupted to Machakos) was a thriving trading centre and it became the principal upcountry administrative centre of the British. Masaku moved to Kangundo in disgust. (His grandson, Paul Ngei, was prominent in the struggle for Kenya's independence.) However, with the arrival of the Europeans so soon after rinderpest had decimated their herds, and with the building of the Uganda Railway and the ban on further expansion into the vacant lands of Ulu and Yatta, the Kamba were soon in economic trouble. Their land was no longer fertile. Their refusal to reduce their herds and the erosion of the impoverished soil led to periods of famine.

Skilled craftsmen with many materials, the Kamba use iron and copper wire to make bracelets, necklets, arrow-heads and spears, and the same skills serve to create inlaid stools of exceptional symmetry and beauty: the Kamba traditional art of wood-carving is the basis of a major handicraft industry, with significant local and export sales. Clay cooking pots are made by the women, as are the finely plaited baskets (*chondo*, pl. *vyondo*) made from fibres of the baobab and wild fig trees. Numerous kinds of animal traps are also constructed.

Smaller than the clans and sub-clans, the basic unit of Kamba life, economic, political, religious and social, is the extended family (*musyi*). Political power, as with many Bantu peoples in Kenya, used to lie in the hands of the elders (*atumia*) and in village or clan meetings (*mbai*). When this system was destroyed by the British at the end of the nineteenth century, appointed leaders such as Chief Kasina Ndoo were imposed, although the concept was foreign to Kamba tradition.

Both sexes undergo circumcision. In parts of Ukambani, there are two stages – the 'small' ceremony (*nzaikonini*) and the 'big' ceremony (*nzaikoneni*) – the first when the child is four to five years of age and the latter at puberty. The

Above: Young Kamba girl with gourd used, in more serious moments, for collecting water.

Opposite: Often hit by drought, natural and man-made reservoirs become a vital year round source for many Kamba who live in the arid areas of Kitui and Machakc Districts.

Below: Calabash sellers in Kitui making water dippers out of defective gourds.

Opposite: Sugar cane stems carpet the floor of a Kamba market. When crushed the cane provides a fermenting juice for home brews.

Bottom: Chicken seller brings fluttery life to rural market-place in Kitui.

nzaikoneni involves a prolonged period of initiation. Once, the Kamba sharpened the incisor teeth in the upper jaw to a point. They used to fashion false teeth from those of ox or hartebeest to replace the ones lost. They also scarified the chest and abdomen for ornamentation. In former days, up to 100 goats (paid in instalments) was not excessive for a rich man's son to pay as bride wealth for the girl of his choice. Cattle, beer, gourds of ghee and bunches of bananas were also given to complete the marriage transaction.

Traditional weapons of the Kamba are the bow and arrow, the ubiquitous long fighting sword (*simi*) and the throwing club. Kamba arrows are finely made and usually poisoned, the iron point being carefully wrapped in a pliable piece of thin leather to keep the poison moist, thereby ensuring optimum effectiveness and also protection against accidental injury. The Kamba are skilled trackers and fearless elephant hunters.

Unlike the neighbouring Kikuyu, the Kamba were slow to adopt progressive agricultural methods, preferring service either in the police and King's African Rifles or on European farms to the work of developing their own land holdings. Government-instituted bench terracing and clearing of tsetse-infected bush were boycotted, reducing, it is said, one British District Commissioner to tears! The principal changes in the social and economic life of the Kamba resulted from the introduction of cash crops, cotton, tobacco and coffee as well as small-scale horticulture. Maize, chick-peas, cowpeas, gourd crops and cassava have been added to the traditional sorghums and millets. Cattle, sheep, goats and chickens are kept. Market days in Ukambani are colourful affairs.

Drought and famine still plague the Kamba people, especially in Kitui. Government and 'Harambee' water and integrated development projects are receiving priority but the further desiccation of Ukambani as a result of poor agricultural practices and deforestation arising from charcoal production (for domestic use or sale in Nairobi and Mombasa) continues to militate against economic development in the area.

Keiyo
SOUTHERN NILOTIC

One of the Kalenjin peoples, the Keiyo probably migrated to their present homeland from the Mount Elgon area some time in the late sixteenth and early seventeenth centuries. Today they live on the virtually inaccessible ledges of the precipitous Elgeyo Escarpment which drops, often with outcrops of exposed rock, 700 metres or more to the gorge of the river Kerio. At one time the Keiyo herded their stock across the rich grasslands of the eastern Uasin Gishu plateau but, harassed by raiding Karamoja and others in the last century, they were forced to seek refuge below the escarpment. Early Swahili caravans and European explorers, including the infamous German Carl Peters, came into occasional conflict with them there.

The Keiyo are nearly all domiciled in the escarpment area, which is some eighty kilometres long and averages no more than twelve to sixteen kilometres in width. Here, as best they can, they till small plots of *wimbi*, millet and maize to augment their traditional milk and blood diet. Only in recent decades have the Keiyo been able to descend from their mountain refuge to cultivate the more fertile lands along the valley floor. The administrative centre, formerly Tambach, is now Iten.

Many Keiyo are agriculturalists, of sheer necessity, but cattle remain their first love. Inoculation programmes and dipping today control such diseases as rinderpest, black-quarter and East Coast fever – against which the Keiyo had evolved their own traditional methods of insurance. In the past, they often deposited a number of their cattle with relatives and friends in different parts of the district. If one locality was stricken with rinderpest it was hoped that the balance of the herd in another area would remain unaffected.

Keiyo legend recalls a noteworthy feat when a raiding party returning from an attack on the Tuken was ambushed before reaching the ford over the Kerio. Left with no alternative but to leap across the five-metre chasm, thirty of the party reached safety. The rest paid the price of failure: a Tuken spear, drowning, or death on the rocks fifteen metres below. It is said that one warrior even succeeded in prodding a captured heifer into making the leap to safety with him.

Keiyo warriors fashion their own accoutrements, but the iron parts of the weapons are forged by smiths. In former days they smelted down ore obtained from known deposits, but latterly they have used either iron ingots or scrap metal. Smiths were looked upon with awe and fear, rather like the alchemists of Medieval Europe. Keiyo smiths are a separate clan, their skills being handed down generation by generation. Keiyo weapons consist of a two-metre spear, shield, bow and arrows and a fighting knife. The bow is commonly made of wood of the *silip* (*mukeo – Dombeya goetzenii*) tree, the bow-string of tendons from the back of an ox. The bow is bent to shape over a hot flame and rubbed smooth with sand. Arrows are usually barbed and often poisoned. The 60-centimetre double-edged fighting knife, common to many of Kenya's people, is worn in a sheath hanging from a belt around the waist. The knife has a wooden handle, which is covered with ox-hide, as is the wooden sheath made from the *teldet* (*mununga – Ekebergia rueppeliana*) tree. For the sheath, the ox-hide is dyed red, boiled and sewn around the wood when still wet and soft.

Game laws and conservation programmes have virtually ended Keiyo opportunities for hunting – at which the courageous were adept, especially at taking elephant, buffalo and rhinoceros for meat. Parties on foot drove the elephant herds into ambushes set by spear-throwing warriors concealed in trees. Leopards were hunted for their skins and to reduce the number of these predators which snatch small stock at night and, not infrequently, take a sheep or goat in broad daylight.

Like the neighbouring Marakwet farther to the north, the Keiyo traditionally site their low, round, thatched huts on virtually inaccessible ledges along the

Above: Traditional Keiyo flour-making with hand pestles used to grind seed crops like millet and maize.

Opposite: Robed in a leather apron, a young Keiyo girl from the Kerio valley of Kenya undergoes initiation for womanhood. Men are forbidden to mix with the candidates. The leather hood and circumcision dress signify her status – and enforce the taboo.

escarpment, which provides a refuge from marauding bands and a healthier environment than the malarial valley of the Kerio river. A thorn fence around the huts gives a night shelter for cattle, sheep and goats. Women milk the cows, using gourds as milk containers. These are first washed out with a little water or cow's urine and then 'sterilised', when dry, by rubbing a burning brand of olive wood around the inside, the embers and large pieces of charcoal being emptied out of the gourd before use. Cows are milked before the cattle are allowed out of the night enclosure.

Earthenware pots supplement gourds for household purposes. The Keiyo augment their own small supply by buying from the neighbouring Marakwet. Pots are built up from rings of clay, smoothed on both sides, first with the fingers and then with a small piece of wood. Handles are added and the pots are dried in the shade for several weeks before being fired.

Honey plays an important part in the economy of the Keiyo, particularly in the southern part of the district. Efforts to establish a viable commercial industry in honey and beeswax have met with little success, for the honey from the hollow-log hives is mainly used to make honey beer or eaten, often mixed with dried and pounded flying ants (termites).

The Keiyo practise both circumcision and clitoridectomy. The girls convalesce in rigid seclusion (*soiyet*) for a month, tended only by older women. During this time they wear a leather hood and no male friends are permitted to see them. Later they are permitted to walk about, but wear a special dress and cover their faces with leather masks. After three months they re-enter everyday life, discard their wooden ear-rings for brass ones and put on the costume of adult women. Traditionally, girls are married shortly afterwards.

The Keiyo were among the first to take up paid employment as herdsmen on the European farms of the Uasin Gishu; others became carpenters and general handymen. The Second World War gave many new opportunities and the military tradition continues today in the Army, police and the Kenya Prisons Service. Keiyo athletes have made their mark in distance running. Population pressures are great and today increasing numbers of Keiyo seek employment outside their home district.

Above: A veteran Keiyo herdsman in the Kerio valley demonstrates how his forebears once protected their herds from marauding outlaws and the stealth of the leopard.

Kikuyu
CENTRAL BANTU

Largest of all Kenya's ethnic groups, the Kikuyu migrated to their present homeland in the Central Province districts of Nyeri (Gaki), Murang'a (Metumi) and Kiambu to the west and south of Mount Kenya (Kirinyaga) from Meru and Tharaka via Mbeere, Mwea and Ndia some 400 years ago. Formerly separate tribes, the Ndia and Gichugu of Kirinyaga District now count themselves as Kikuyu. The Kikuyu number 3,203,000. More romantically, the legendary founder of the tribe was the man Gikuyu. Taken to the summit of Kirinyaga by the Divine Spirit *Ngai* he was commanded to establish his homestead near a cluster of fig trees (*mikuyu*) in the centre of the country. There *Ngai* had provided for him a beautiful wife, Mumbi. From their nine daughters originated the principal clans.

Kikuyu tribal organisation is based on the family (*nyumba*). Several families make up a homestead (*mucii*) of a sub-group (*mbari*) and clan (*muhiriga*) of which there are nine major groupings: Achera, Agachiku, Airimu, Ambui, Angare, Anjiru, Angui, Aithaga, and Aitherandu (many Kikuyu add a tenth clan, although claiming there to be nine, for to count children, people or livestock is thought to bring misfortune).

Circumcision was a prerequisite for youths to join the ranks of the warriors (*anake*) who graduated to the council of elders (*kiama*) and a select few of whom composed the secret council known as *njama*. The *kiama* was responsible for the settlement of disputes. If the elders were baffled as to the guilt of those involved, the case could be settled by the ordeal of the hot knife (innocence or guilt being determined by the extent of blistering of the tongue) or an oath taken on the feared seven-holed *githathi* stone.

Formerly the two Kikuyu generation-sets, Maina and Mwangi, alternately held power for periods of thirty years or more. The handing-over ceremony (*ituika*) signified the retirement of a generation-set, who were then given a specific name commemorating some outstanding feature of their period of authority. Kikuyu oral tradition recalls a number of generation-set names in the Iregi, Ndemi, Ciira, Mathathi, Cuma, Chororo and Choka (Manduti, Agu and Tene have also been noted).

The Kikuyu expanded throughout and burned and cleared the dense forests of what is now Central Province by purchase, blood-brotherhood and intermarriage with the original hunter-gatherer inhabitants of the area, the now extinct Athi and Gumba and, especially in the southern Nyandarua mountains, the Okiek. A Kikuyu man unable to purchase land in his own right sought uncultivated land to till on a tenant (*muhoi*, pl. *ahoi*) basis. Land is a dominant factor in the social, political, religious and economic life of these agriculturalists and brought them into early conflict with the European settlers who had alienated areas of Kikuyuland for their own use.

Cattle, formerly a status symbol indicative of a man's wealth, provided economic benefits too – hides for bedding, sandals and carrying straps (*mukwa*, pl. *mikwa*). Sheep and goats (*mburi*) were, and still are, used for various religious sacrifices and purifications. Permanent crops such as bananas, sugar cane, arum lily (*nduma*) and yams (*gikwa*, pl. *ikwa*), together with beans, millet (*mwere*), maize, sweet potatoes, a variety of vegetables and black beans (*njahi*), form the staples of the Kikuyu diet.

Kikuyu crafts include the making of pots for cooking, carrying and storing water and storage of grains and other produce. Pots were also a major item of barter. Woven baskets (*kiondo*, pl. *ciondo*) are made from a variety of fibres, originally obtained from the bark of shrubs, more recently of sisal or synthetic thread. Flat trays (*gitaruru*, pl. *itaruru*) are woven from the bark of the *mugu*, *mugiyo* and *muthuthi* shrubs. Arrow-heads, spears, swords, cowbells, rattles and tweezers were manufactured by blacksmiths (*muturi*, pl. *aturi*) who were believed to have magical abilities.

Above: The distinctive ear-rings of a Kikuyu elder indicate his status in the community and membership the select council, kiama kia maturanguru.

Opposite: Proud in the insignia of office, a Kikuyu chie attends Kenya's Independence Day celebrations in a colourful mixture of dress, national and modern.

Livestock, agricultural produce and iron implements, tobacco, salt and ochre were bartered at local markets held at regular intervals in the more densely populated areas of Kikuyuland. Important centres of trade were Karatina, Gacatha and Gakindu in Gaki, and Muthithi and Giitwa in Murang'a. Trading contacts were also maintained with the neighbouring Maasai, Kamba and Okiek, and the caravans of women who transported goods for barter were immune from molestation, usually under the protection of a 'middleman' (*hinga*) related to the group with which they intended to trade.

A traumatic confrontation between tribal leaders anxious to preserve their cultural heritage and the European missionaries occurred in the late 1920s over the socio-religious rite of clitoridectomy (*irua*) of girls. Disaffection with the missionary stance led to the establishment of the Kikuyu Independent Schools Association (KISA) and the Kikuyu Karing'a (Pure) Educational Association out of which evolved the African Pentecostal Church and the African Orthodox Church – independent church movements based on the Old Testament (which nowhere condemns female circumcision and refers to polygamous marriages).

Perhaps better than any other tribe, the Kikuyu adapted to the challenge of Western culture, and displayed an early political awareness that resulted in the formation of the Kikuyu Association in 1920 which was soon drawing up a petition of grievances to present to the Chief Native Commissioner. Forced labour, land expropriation, the *kipande* system and the lack of public services and educational opportunities were to remain the basic African grievances until the end of the colonial era. Early political leaders included Harry Thuku, James Beauttah and Johnstone (Jomo) Kenyatta. The Kikuyu Central Association of the mid-1920s was banned in 1940, but replaced after the Second World War by the broader-based, national Kenya African Union. Kenyatta returned in 1946 from sixteen years of exile in Britain to lead the drive for independence. He was imprisoned when a State of Emergency was declared in 1952 to counter the Mau Mau freedom movement. Independence was finally won on December 12, 1963, and Jomo Kenyatta (*c.* 1896–1978) was sworn in as the first President of the Republic of Kenya a year later.

Today, on economic holdings consolidated from fragments of former tribal lands, progressive Kikuyu farmers have benefited from modern agricultural practices and the upgrading of their livestock, the accessible markets of Nairobi and a growing export trade in coffee, tea, pyrethrum, horticultural crops and flowers and have emerged as Kenya's major farming community. They also command much of the farmlands of the former White Highlands and are active in business and commerce throughout Kenya. About 400,000 Kikuyu make their home in Nairobi (40 per cent of the city's population) and they form a significant proportion of the populations of other Kenya towns.

Above: Young Kikuyu girl with baby brother.

Kipsigis
SOUTHERN NILOTIC

Numerically the Kipsigis are the largest of the Kalenjin (literally, 'I tell you') people, who together total 1,652,000, and live in the Rift Valley of western Kenya speaking different dialects of the same language. Others of the Kalenjin group, who share a common political affinity and customs, are the Nandi, Tuken, Marakwet, Keiyo, Pokot, Terik and Sabaot (comprising the Kony, Bok and Bongomek of Mount Elgon). The Kipsigis occupy the southernmost part of Kalenjin territory, of which Kericho is the administrative centre.

Agriculturalists, the Kipsigis (or Lumbwa, as they were once known) have a passionate love of cattle, and cattle raids across their borders with the Gusii, Luo and Maasai were and still are a recurring source of friction. The Kipsigis traditionally claim to have migrated to their present homeland from *Tto* far to the north, perhaps in the area of the Kenya–Sudan border, or even *Misri* (Egypt). Legend has it that *Tto* was an arid region. One evening when the men were gathered around their fires bewailing the lack of grazing for their cattle, a bat (*reresiet*) appeared with a blade of grass in its mouth. This was considered a good omen and the bat was followed southwards until the Kipsigis came to a fertile land. Mount Elgon and the area around Lake Baringo were probable resting stages before the Kipsigis reached the fertile uplands, between 1,200 and 1,500 metres, that are now their home and from which they ousted the Sirikwa, a Kalenjin group who had preceded them in the area.

The strength of the Kipsigis was in their four organised military units (*poriosiek*) of Kipkaige, Ngetunyo, Kebeni and Kasanet. Initially each unit raided independently of the others, but later they were welded into one formidable army capable of expanding tribal territory and containing their surrounding enemies, including the powerful Maasai.

The Kipsigis have seven major age-sets (*ipinwek*) – Sawe, Chuma, Maina, Nyongi, Kipnyige, Kaplelach and Kipkoimet (or Korongoro) – which are recalled in order. Every age-set is composed of three, sometimes four, sub-sets. The period of time that elapses between the initiation of the sub-sets is usually seven years. Each age-set thus covers a period of some twenty-one years, and it takes roughly 147 years for all seven age-sets to be recalled and a new cycle started. The period of initiation may last between four and eight months, and is the critical point in the life of the initiates, both boys and girls. Circumcision is only the first of a series of ceremonies and instructions into the customs and traditions of the tribe. Initiation usually starts at harvest time. Large quantities of grain are required to brew beer, for relations and friends come from all parts to join in the ceremonies. Girls marry immediately they complete the initiation rites.

There are many clans (*ortinwek*), and the relationship between the members of each one is symbolised by a totem, usually an animal. For example, the totem of the Konganyot clan is the crested crane and that of the Peliot clan the elephant. Other groupings of importance, which overlap and interact with each other, are the social group *kokwotinwek* and the family.

The Kipsigis backed the Nandi when they resisted the advance of the Europeans, raiding the railway camp at Fort Ternan (1902) and making many attacks thereafter on neighbouring tribes friendly to the British administration, who responded with punitive measures. An administrative post was established at Sotik in 1905 and a buffer zone of some 2,000 hectares, between the Kipsigis and the Gusii, was parcelled out to European settlers. The chief ritual expert (*orkoiyot*) Arap Koilegei was deported to Nyeri in 1913 prior to being transferred to Meru, where he later died.

Wimbi is grown on newly cultivated land. Traditionally it played an important part in the Kipsigis way of life, both for the brewing of beer (which the Kipsigis drink from a communal pot through tubes two to four metres long, made from the *rogoret* creeper), and for *kimiet*, a dish similar to *ugali*, which may

Above and opposite: Two young Kipsigis girls prepare for the intricate rituals which will lead them to marriage. They walk from their home in Kapkimolwa in Kericho District, in the distinctive initiation dress of blackened skins, ornamented with clusters of bamboo beads, to the nearby home of an old woman where they will be counselled in their people's virtues and take part in the secret ritual of rotyinotet, *followed by clitoridectomy. The initiation culminates in a series of ceremonies, one known as the opening of the way to womanhood,* yatet ap orot, *and another as the cutting of the stick,* tilet ap, *and the shaving of the head. Thus prepared, the young girls emerge as women,* chebkeleyot, *and are married virtually at once.*

Below: Clothed in traditional skin robes, a pensive Kipsigis cattle owner keeps guard over his herd – a vital source of wealth, prestige and sustenance including milk, meat and blood.

Above: A sack of maize on her head, a young Kipsigis mother heads for the village mill where she will grind the maize into flour for cooking. At the birth of a child, the women of the homestead call on the father to give blood – bull's blood for a boy, cow's blood for a girl. The child's first name, kurenet, *commemorates a deed or physical characteristic of an ancestor.*

be eaten with curdled milk or cooked vegetables. The Kipsigis grow a number of cash crops, especially tea and pyrethrum. Vegetables (potatoes, maize, cabbage, tomatoes, onions, peas and beans) are grown in addition to traditional crops such as bananas and sweet potatoes. Increasing numbers of grade cattle are being maintained on their well-kept small-holdings and they are one of Kenya's leading farming communities.

The Kalenjin, and especially the Nandi and Kipsigis, are renowned as athletes, and many of Kenya's world-famous track stars have been Kipsigis. Notable among these has been Wilson Kiprigut Chuma, who won a bronze medal in the 800 metres in Tokyo in 1964, Kenya's first ever Olympic award.

Opposite: Kipsigis working in a Buret quarry where deep scars etch the red sandstone hills. Sand for building work is obtained by crushing the sandstone into fine particles.

Kuria
WESTERN BANTU

The Kuria (89,000) live astride the Kenya–Tanzania border on the cooler, higher ground south of Kisii to the east of Lake Victoria, but separated from the lake region by a wedge of formerly Bantu-speaking Suba and the Luo. Even now there are few access roads to this hilly area in South Nyanza with its deeply cut valleys and swift-flowing streams.

Of diverse origins, the Kuria (or Watende) are an amalgam of assimilated Gusii clans from the north (the Abakira, the Aba-Nyabaasi and the Aba-Sweta), and of the Abagumbe from the Chepalungu area close to the present Maasai/Kipsigis border (with the Aba-Kungu, Aba-Irege and other Bantu groups) in their present homeland. In all they comprise some seventeen clans. The most marked physical characteristic of the Kuria used to be their chipped teeth, chopped and filed to points. Two of the top teeth were removed.

The Kuria live in fortified family homesteads, often clustered close together but, since land demarcation, sited on individual holdings. A thick fence (masancho) of branches and poles connects the individual huts (nyumba) of the homestead and provides a cattle yard (obori) which can be easily defended from Maasai and Kipsigis raiders. Small grain stores (iritara), of woven baskets plastered on the inside with dung and mud, opened by tilting the thatched roofs, stand next to the homestead. Unmarried sons live in a special hut (isiga).

The loamy soils combine with a high, well-dispersed rainfall to provide fertile conditions for agriculture, and the Kuria grow a variety of subsistence and cash crops: sweet potatoes, finger millet, maize, cassava and bananas and vegetables. Pyrethrum, coffee and, more recently, tobacco bring in useful cash incomes from the comparatively large individual holdings, many of which exceed twenty hectares. Dual purpose cattle are the principal livestock, although sheep and goats are also kept. Newly introduced Swahili bulls are upgrading the beef and dairy herds.

Circumcision garments (ichisusume) set apart the young men of the tribe who are initiated in groups of several hundred. After passing through a month-long series of ceremonies and ritual smearings with white clay the initiates attend a symbolic washing (ibihwi) to rank finally as abamura – men. Girl initiates (abasagane) receive recognition of their new status and womanhood with the term abaiseke. Thereafter, men are eligible to marry. Negotiations for a bride are opened by the young man's uncle (somoke), who discusses bride wealth (ikihingo) on his behalf. The groom and bride each sleep a night in the other's homestead before the day the bride is taken to the sacred shrine of stones for the ritual of isumbo. In this ceremony she is expected to rid herself of all the evil she has caused in her life. The same evening, after the final payment of the dowry, she is escorted to her husband's home by his sister.

Complicated rules govern the payment of the bride wealth, usually calculated as five to twenty cows. Ikihingo, the main dowry payment made prior to the marriage, contrasts with ekebete, intermittent payments made during the girl's early years against her attainment of womanhood and marriage. Such payments may start before she has even stopped suckling. Should the arranged marriage fail to materialise, the girl's father is faced with returning not only the cattle he has accepted in payment but also all the calves. Should the bride die before isumbo is completed all the dowry is returned with the exception of one cow; should she die after a year or more without child half the dowry is returned, but nothing is demanded if she has already had a child. Cousins are not allowed to marry (mubiara wi biinyanone).

The young men of the Kuria call meetings of their age-mates to discuss common problems, and communal tasks (isiri) are often carried out by the young men and women. In the past, frequent cattle raids against neighbouring enemies were encouraged. The leader (umunchiria) of the raiding party (iriko) gained fame and honour if they succeeded in running off Maasai and Kipsigis

Above: A colourfully robed girl of the Kuria people wh live south-east of Lake Victoria and who are divided in two great families, the Abachuma *and* Abasai. *Leger has it that these names derive from the younger and older wives of the tribe's founder,* Mokuria.

Opposite: Height and status enhanced by wooden clog a Kuria dancer leads three young girls in a traditional dance routine. Plucked eyebrows are regarded as a sigr of womanly beauty and not too long ago both men and women pierced and elongated the ear-lobes with woode plugs.

cattle. When threatened with common problems the clan elders meet (*inina ki ritongo*) to discuss the matter on a collective basis.

Death, it is believed, results from two causes: divine intervention (*amasambo*) and ancestors (*ibihwi*). The gods are appeased by the slaughter of goats and cows at a sacred shrine and a sacred stone (*ukwikaga*) is carried to protect the holder from harm. The dead are appeased by being offered something they had favoured when alive. Traditionally, men and women were buried naked, the man to the right of his home and the woman to the left. An exceptionally rich man owning many cattle is buried in the hide of a bull slaughtered for the purpose. During the four to five days of mourning, near relatives shave their heads and if married ritually cleanse themselves at the end of this period by slaughtering a goat (*ukwirabia*), or if single by smearing their bodies with flour (*ekeraba*).

Renowned for the vigorous dances of their young, bare-breasted girls, whose male partners wear wooden clogs (*imitiambwe*) twenty to thirty centimetres thick (unique in Kenya) carved from the *umuriba* tree, the Kuria celebrate many occasions. Circumcision and marriage are enlivened by dances. *Induru* and *isururu* are danced at the elevation of elders to higher status within the clan. Large wooden ear-plugs were once worn by the young women and the youths, too, fixed a large rounded wooden block into both ear-lobes, so that it dangled behind the neck or on to the chest. A wide range of musical instruments provides the accompaniment to dances and in special cases the songs of outstanding musicians. Commonly, the eight-stringed bowl lyre (*iritingo*), with a stick of metal rattles (*ibituriani*) sounded with the foot, is used. Talented minstrels were, and are, in demand to play at weddings, other feasts and celebrations. The drum (*embegete*), played with the hands from a kneeling position, and the gourds (*ibirandi*) filled with seeds of the *ororara* tree are used to provide the rhythm. The flute (*induru*) and the war horn (*irirongwe*), made from an eland horn, are the two main wind instruments. The latter's deep booming note alerts neighbours that a raid is in progress and that their help is required to repulse the enemy.

The Kuria, the larger section of which lives across the border in Tanzania, quickly responded to the impetus given by education, and many primary and secondary schools exist throughout Kuria territory: in the last three decades a quiet revolution has taken place in the development of the economy. The large holdings are well planned and tended, and the small townships of Ntimaru, Nyabasi, Taraganya and Kihancha provide not only market-places and venues for social activities but are rapidly becoming centres for diversified trading activities and craft workshops.

Above: Large beaded ear-rings are attractive replacements for the cumbersome wooden plugs this Kuria woman wore in her youth.

Luo
WESTERN NILOTIC

Largest of the non-Bantu ethnic groups in Kenya (1,956,000), the Luo of Central and South Nyanza districts, around the Kavirondo Gulf of Lake Victoria, represent the most vigorous of successive southward drives of Nilotes from the Sudan. The administrative centre is Kisumu.

The Luo are related to Nilotic peoples far beyond the borders of Kenya: to the Mesarit and Daju of Chad; the Dinka of Sudan and Central African Republic; the Nuer, Bor, Beri and Shilluk of Sudan; the Anuak of Sudan and Ethiopia; the Jonaam and Alur of Zaire and Uganda; and to the Acholi, Lango and Padhola of Uganda. The first wave of Luo immigrants probably arrived in Nyanza at least five centuries ago, driving out or assimilating the Bantu occupants of the region. The arrival of the last of the Luo groups in the eighteenth century coincided with the thrust into South Nyanza, causing the Gusii, Kuria and Suba to retreat and bringing the Luo into contact with the Maasai and Kipsigis. Four major groups, the Joka-Jok, Joka-Owiny, Joka-Omolo and Joka-Suba, make up these Dholuo-speaking peoples, who claim common descent from the mythological patriarch Ramogi, supposedly the founder of the first Luo settlement on a hill in Kadimu.

Cattle and constant migrations in search of pastures for their herds dominated the life of the first Luo immigrants. But further expansion eastward was blocked and their herds were decimated by rinderpest. The Luo adjusted to growing population pressures by adopting a sedentary way of life in relatively isolated homesteads. Although cattle continued to dominate ritual and economic activities, agriculture and fishing became increasingly important for subsistence. Sorghum, sim-sim and finger millet were the traditional crops grown, and now vegetables, groundnuts, coffee and sugar cane are valuable additions in a cash economy.

Nonetheless, these people of the lakes and rivers have maintained their migratory instincts. They say of themselves: the Luo are like water, which flows until it finds its own level. And indeed tens of thousands of Luo seeking employment have flooded the major towns of Kenya, especially Nairobi and Mombasa.

Foremost among Kenya's people in their fishing skills, the Luo today mainly use gill nets and long-line fishing to catch tilapia (*ngege*) and other fish. If the bell-shaped baskets (once used by groups of Luo women) and the papyrus *ngogo* seine-type nets are no longer employed, extensive use is still made of basket traps, either on their own or in conjunction with the *osageru* fish maze and the *kek* river fence and its modification the *obalala* at the mouths of rivers. For poling along in the shallows of Lake Victoria, the Luo formerly used crude log and 'bundle' rafts of papyrus or saplings. In deeper water, hollowed-out log canoes or plank-built craft of considerable complexity and size are employed. Introduced on Lake Victoria by the Arabs, the dhow-type fishing boats used in offshore fishing seem to have been first constructed on the Winam Gulf by Asians and later adapted and built by the Luo themselves, leading to more intensive exploitation of the fisheries in the Winam Gulf and north and south along the shores of the open lake. The more advanced Ssesse canoe of the Baganda has also been adopted and many are now moulded in fibre-glass. Powered by outboard motors, the canoes are extensively used not only by the Luo fishermen of Lake Victoria but on most of Kenya's inland waters.

The head of a Luo homestead has his own hut (*duol*) built near the cattle enclosure, and it is here that important matters relating to the household and community are discussed among the clan elders. Wives have their individual huts and may not sleep in the *duol*. Traditionally, a young woman whose suitor had paid sufficient bride wealth to the parents would be seized and carried off by force by the bridegroom and his friends. A number of ceremonies followed upon this abduction (*meko*), culminating in the feast (*riso*) given by the husband for

Above and opposite: Hand-woven basket traps are one the main forms of fishing for the Luo of Lake Victoria. Fishermen arrange the traps into a kind of fish maze, osageru, *at the mouth of one of the many streams which flow into the lake.*

Below: Relaxing at her market stall, a Luo pineapple vendor contentedly smokes her pipe. Most Luo matrons nowadays smoke cigarettes, often back to front with the lighted end inside the mouth!

Opposite: For centuries trade between the lowland Luo and the upland Gusii has flourished. A donkey caravan hauls cattle salt, from Kendu Bay on the shores of Lake Victoria, up a hillside track in lush Gusii country to barter for maize.

his relatives. Today, traditional bride wealth requirements are often met by a cash payment in lieu of cattle and marriages are formalised by Christian rite.

Expectant mothers observe certain customs and dietary taboos. A new-born child may have cold water poured over it to make it cry, or tobacco smoke blown up its nose. Twins are considered especially unfavourable. The Luo practise neither circumcision nor clitoridectomy, although a growing number of young boys now undergo circumcision either for religious reasons (male members of the Nomiya Luo Church and Luo Muslims) or to conform to the widely accepted belief of many Kenyans that this operation is the mark of manhood.

The ancestors of the Luo play a vital role in the spiritual life of the community, and the spirits of the truly great – Gor Mahia, Ramogi, and Lwanda Magere – continue to be revered. The good spirits (*nyasaye*, pl. *nyiseche*), however, have to contend with a host of hostile cousins (*jochiende*) and wizards (*jajuok*). Witchcraft flourished (and is far from eradicated) on the fringes of this 'shadow' world. Its practitioners were summoned to wreak vengeance by subtle artifice on real or imagined enemies, employing a whole range of techniques from the 'evil eye' to the 'willing' of misfortune or death.

An articulate, community-conscious people, the Luo were prominent in the struggle for independence during the colonial regime. They provided many leading trade unionists and politicians, of whom the late Tom Mboya (assassinated in 1969) and the former Vice-President of Kenya, Oginga Odinga, fanned the flame of *Uhuru* (Independence). Luo folklore has been imaginatively captured in the modern fiction of Grace Ogot and Tom Okoyo.

Above: Luo dancers decorated in vivid colours and wearing ostrich feathers, hippo teeth, cow and impala horns. The same materials form the regalia of Luo prophets and warriors and are incorporated in funeral masks.

Luyia
WESTERN BANTU

Seventeen sub-tribes make up the Abaluyia peoples (2,120,000) of western Kenya. These are the Bukusu (derisively referred to by their neighbours as the Kitosh), Tachoni, Kabrasi, Kakalewa (Bunyala), Butsotso, Isukha (Kakumega), Idakho, Tiriki, Maragoli, Wanga, Marama, Kisa, Nyala, Bukhayo (Xaiyo), Marachi, Samia and Bunyore (Nyore). The administrative centre is Kakamega. Population density between Kisumu and Kakamega (over 750 to the square kilometre) is one of the highest in rural Africa.

The word Abaluyia derives from the word *oluyia* (communal courtyard), for out of the customary clan gatherings around the evening fires arose the practice of quizzing a newcomer with the expression 'To which *oluyia* do you belong'? As an all-embracing term for this group of sub-tribes sharing cultural, linguistic and political affinities 'Abaluyia' only came into general usage from 1940 when the Baluyia Welfare Association was formed.

Traditional claims to an origin in *Misri* (Egypt) can be discounted. The earliest Luyia settlement in the area probably began around the fourteenth and continued into the seventeenth century: almost certainly part of a steady eastward drift from present-day Zaire or western Uganda. Other sub-tribes of the group may have come from the south, and those in the Mount Elgon region arrived from the north more recently. Legend has it that the Luyia people are descendants of *Wele* (often spelt *Were*, and meaning God). *Wele* created a boy and a girl, say the Bukusu, who were called Akuru and Muka: they bore two children, Mugoma and his sister Malaba. From these two couples stem the various Luyia sub-tribes.

The Wanga formerly recognised a hereditary chief ruler, the *Nabongo*. On the death of the reigning *Nabongo*, his successor had to kill a cow ceremonially with the royal spear which the dynasty had brought with it from '*Misri*'. Supported by Maasai mercenaries and in the last decades of the eighteenth century armed with guns bought from Swahili ivory traders, the Wanga Empire expanded rapidly – and declined almost as quickly. Joseph Thomson was the first European to make contact with the last *Nabongo*, Mumia. He came to power in the early 1880s, proved a friend of the British who endeavoured without success to extend Wanga rule to all Luyia, and was almost one hundred years old when he died in 1949.

Until recently, Luyia villages (*litala*, pl. *amatala*) were usually surrounded by euphorbia hedges, although larger settlements protected by clay walls and defensive ditches (*olukoba*, pl. *tsingoba*) were not uncommon in areas where there was likelihood of raids by the Nandi, Iteso and Maasai. Agriculturalists, the Luyia also kept cattle, sheep, goats and chickens. Sorghum and finger millet, sweet potatoes and pumpkins and several varieties of beans were grown. Termites and locusts were considered delicacies.

The Luyia were avid hunters, employing baited traps and snares, nets and pits. Large hunting parties, armed with spears and bows and arrows, and accompanied by packs of dogs, took their toll of smaller game. Children caught birds using a sticky vegetable paste spread on twigs. Trophies from the hunt – colobus monkey skins, giraffe and zebra tails, ostrich feathers and warthog tusks – were and still are used for ceremonial robes, bracelets, fly whisks and decorative head-dresses.

The Samia were the most skilled of Luyia smelters and workers in iron, and the hoes, knives and other implements which they forged were used as a form of currency over a wide area. The making of pots and baskets of all types (used for fishing along the shores of Lake Victoria and the lower reaches of the Yala, Nzoia and Sio rivers) is still a common craft.

Circumcision was not formerly practised by all Luyia peoples, but where this rite was performed an age-group (*likhula*) would be initiated together. The removal of four or six teeth from the lower jaw would also be carried out on an

Above, opposite and overleaf: Notable fishermen and boat builders (above) exist among the Bunyala and Samia of Port Victoria and Sio in western Kenya on eastern shore of Lake Victoria. The sandy beaches of Sunba Channel (opposite) by mid-morning are bright with the colourful skeins of nets drying in the sun and (following page) emblazoned canoes hauled out to dry.

age-group basis. The young initiates then left their parents' hut for the communal *isimba* hut. Arranged marriages were not uncommon among the Luyia, although a young man could also obtain the consent of a girl of his choice. A go-between (*wangira*) was often used by the parents of the boy and girl to enquire into the suitability of the match. Bride wealth (*obukhwe*) was usually paid in instalments, from three to twenty cattle or their equivalent in goats and iron hoes. Each set of parents maintained a tally of the payments with bundles of marked sticks. Today, bride wealth is paid in cash.

Most Luyia sub-tribes acquiesced to the 'new order' when the British took over the administration of the Uganda Protectorate (of which the area was once part). However, bitter and bloody fighting resulted before the Bukusu and Kakalewa submitted. Machine-gunned out of their fortified villages, they resorted to guerilla action until, harassed and desperate, they were finally massacred in a last stand in Chetambe's fort near Webuye in 1895.

Gold was discovered in Kakamega in 1931, and resulted in an influx of European and African prospectors. The mining companies, at the height of operations in 1935, employed as many as 7,000 Africans. But within a decade the gold was exhausted, and the mainly Luyia labour force dispersed to find jobs on the farms of Trans Nzoia and Uasin Gishu.

Groundnuts, sim-sim and maize, and later cotton, were introduced as cash crops. Today, parts of Western Province are being rapidly developed with the aid of World Bank loans to produce the extra tens of thousands of bales of cotton required by textile mills in Kisumu, Eldoret, Thika and Nanyuki.

Third largest of Kenya's ethnic groupings, the Luyia have two major loves: music and soccer. Shem Chimoto, Elijah Lidonde and Joe Kadenge in past decades have been the stars of both their club and national soccer teams, and AFC Leopards one of the paramount sides in the Kenya National League, an added bond in uniting these once disparate peoples. Luyia politicians of national stature include Masinde Muliro and Elijah Mwangale.

Above: The cheerful smile of a Luyia market girl near Yala, western Kenya. Her name, Nabwire, means 'born at night'. Other common girls' names are Nafula, 'born during rain'; Nekesa, 'born at harvest time'; and Nanjala, 'born during a famine'.

Opposite: Charcoal burning near Butere in Kenya's Western Province. Wattle and eucalyptus trees are the most common species for making charcoal, widely used throughout rural Kenya for cooking. Groves of red hot poker trees (Erythrina abyssinica), an indigenous species known to the Luyia as omutembe, are sacred and thus spared the woodman's axe.

Maasai
EASTERN NILOTIC

The pastoral Maasai (241,500), who share the Olmaa language from which their name derives within Kenya with the Samburu and Ilchamus and with the Arusha and Baraguyu (or Wakwavi) in Tanzania, occupy the Narok and Kajiado districts of Kenya.

A fusion of Nilotic and Cushitic peoples, effected north-west of Lake Turkana a millennium ago, the Maasai ascended the escarpment out of the Kerio Valley and in the ensuing centuries spread across the fertile grasslands of the Rift Valley and surrounding uplands. By the last century, they had established a reputation as powerful and ferocious people: their warrior bands raided hundreds of miles into neighbouring territories to capture the cattle they coveted and, strategically placed across the routes to the lakes, they demanded tribute from the trade caravans and were ignored only by the foolhardy. In the closing years of the nineteenth century, however, the Maasai herds were decimated by rinderpest and drought, and the once united people devastated by inter-section strife. It was a situation which the Government exploited, through the treaties of 1904 and 1911, to move the Maasai out of all their northern grazing lands on Laikipia.

The basic economic and social unit is the *enkang*, a semi-permanent settlement of several families pasturing their stock together, perhaps ten to twenty huts surrounded by a thorn fence, into which enclosure the livestock are driven at night. The warriors' *i-manyat* (each containing perhaps fifty or more huts) are inhabited by all members of one age-set in a district. With them live their mothers and unmarried girls (*en-tito*, pl. *in-toyie*).

Fresh and curdled milk, carried and stored in long, decorated gourds, is the basic item in the Maasai diet. With it may be mixed blood tapped from the jugular vein of a bullock or cow. Sheep and goats are the principal source of meat; cattle are more rarely slaughtered, and then usually for ceremonial purposes. The meat of wild animals is forbidden, with the exception of eland and buffalo.

The Maasai people comprise five (some authorities claim seven) clans: il-makesen, il-aiser, il-molelian, il-taarrosero and il-ikumai. Each is divided into a number of divisions, distinguished by their characteristic cattle brands. These clans are spread throughout Maasailand, although there are individuals who belong to offshoot sections bearing different names. Authority derives from the age-group and the age-set. Prior to circumcision a natural leader or *olaiguenani* is selected; he leads his age-group through a series of rituals until old age, sharing responsibility with a select few, of whom the ritual expert (*oloiboni*) is the ultimate authority.

The last great diviner of the Maasai was Lenana, son of Mbatian, who was the chief *oloiboni* before him. These two are immortalised in the names of the two main peaks of Mount Kenya. Legend has it that as old Mbatian lay on his death bed, he called his eldest son, Sendeyo, to come early next morning as he wished to bequeath to him the powers and instruments of office. Lenana overheard this instruction and, knowing his enfeebled, half-blind father was unable to distinguish him from Sendeyo, forestalled his brother. Unsuspecting, Mbatian handed over to Lenana the iron club, medicine horn, traditional stones and carrying bag. Lenana became the official *oloiboni*. Later a collaborator with the newly arrived Europeans, he acquiesced to the treaties that deprived his people of their lands.

Maasai youths are not circumcised until they are mature, and a new age-set is initiated together at regular intervals of twelve to fifteen years. The young warriors (*il-murran*) remain initiates for some time, using blunt arrows to hunt small birds which are stuffed and tied on to a frame to form a head-dress. Taboos which characterise the life of the warriors include prohibitions on drinking milk in their parents' huts and the eating of meat in the *i-manyat*. Oxen are

Above: Weighed down with head-dress, ear-rings and necklaces a young Maasai girl, en-tito, is free to flirt and befriend a young warrior, ol-murrani, until her circumcision imposes the constraints of womanhood.

Opposite: Famed Maasai lion mane head-dress testifies that the warrior has faced and killed a lion with his spear – a feat now only allowed in defence of cattle.

*Below: Thorn scrub flanks the circular fence of a
traditional Maasai family settlement,* enkang, *in
Kajiado District, southern Kenya.*

slaughtered away from the settlements to provide meat for the warriors, who
carry the long-bladed stabbing spears and buffalo-hide shields with their black,
red and white designs which mark their status. Eventually, in their turn, the
warrior age-set gives way to its juniors and graduates in a special ceremony
(*eunoto*) to senior status.

A warrior of repute without physical blemish and endowed with qualities of
leadership is selected to 'open the way' for the others of his age-set to be
initiated. Once the new age-group leader (*olotuno*) is approved by the *oloiboni*, a
bullock is slaughtered and the leader is the first to drink the blood from the
animal's neck. The enclosure and ceremonial hut built specifically for the
eunoto ceremony is known as *enkang o sinkira*, and it is here that the four days of
rites are staged. Sitting on the same cowhide on which he was circumcised,
each warrior has his head shaved by his mother. The freshly-shaved head is
decorated with a mixture of ochre and fat. At the close of the ceremony the
olotuno is invited to select any girl he chooses for a wife – signalling the next
phase for the newly graduated senior warriors, who are henceforth permitted to
marry. After further rituals, the taboos on the handling and eating of milk and
meat are lifted.

As for centuries past, the life of the Maasai is conditioned by the constant
quest for water and grazing. In the more arid areas of Maasailand, livestock is

Below: Maasai warriors (il-murran) decorate themselves with white clay in preparation for the most significant of their age-group ceremonies, the rites of eunoto.

Opposite: For the eunoto ceremonies a bull is ritually smothered to death, skinned, dismembered and roasted over a glowing wood fire. For each of the elders and initiates finger-rings are cut from the hide and then the meat is taken around the circle of il-murran. Each bit in turn on the meat, the act sealing a life-long bond of fidelity to each of his age-mates.

Above: Maasai herdboy keeps vigil atop a tree stump.

moved seasonally, often several hundred kilometres, to take advantage of undergrazed areas or new growth generated by localised rain. Donkeys are used as pack animals. Cattle are culled and sold to the Kenya Meat Commission at Athi River or to buyers from Nairobi and Nakuru, although most Maasai remain reluctant to reduce their herds to the carrying capacity of the land. Is not cattle wealth given to them by God (*Enkai*)? Group ranching schemes in Kajiado are resulting in the permanent settlement of increasing numbers of Maasai. In Narok, fertile wheatlands on the slopes of the Mau, initially developed by entrepreneurs, are now being exploited by the Maasai themselves. Inevitably, change, long resisted, is now reluctantly accepted.

Marakwet
SOUTHERN NILOTIC

The six territorial groups (from north to south, the Endo, Markweta, Borokot, Almo, Kiptani and to the west the Cherang'any or Sengwer) which make up the Marakwet, more correctly Marakweta, people of the Kerio Valley and the Cherangani Hills of Elgeyo-Marakwet District in Kenya's Rift Valley Province are all members of the Kalenjin group. The administrative centre is Iten.

The Marakwet are divided into 13 clans (Kabon, Moi, Kobil, Mokich, Saniak, Sogom, Sot, Syokwei, Talai, Terik, Tingo, Toyoi and Tul) which cut across the territorial groups. With the exception of the Sogom, each clan is divided into two or more exogamic sections distinguished by totems (for example, Kabon totems are baboon, frog, rat and taiywa, a species of wild fowl).

As a defence against disease and man, for the Kerio Valley is rife with mosquitoes and tsetse fly and was until recently a natural north-south route for raiding parties, the Marakwet traditionally built their houses on the escarpment which in the west rises to 3,370 metres. The Cherangani Hills, rising to over 4,000 metres, with giant groundsels and lobelias on their summits, are particularly rugged and impressive: their eastern wall is one of the highest of all the escarpments that bound the Rift Valley.

The terrain tends to limit stock to sheep and goats, although increasing numbers of cattle are now kept. Crops are grown on the ledges of the escarpment and in the valley, irrigated through 400-year-old furrows running from the Arror, Embebut and Embomen rivers. Of uncertain origin, the furrows are maintained and repaired communally. Traditional staples of diet are eleusine (*wimbi*) and sorghum together with bananas, cassava and maize grown on tilled strips of land (*roran*). Bee-keeping is an important industry among the Cherang'any.

Initiation (*sonok* or *tum*) into eight age-sets prepares the young men and women for adult status within the tribe. The male age-sets are Kaplelach, Nyongi, Chumo, Korongoro, Kimnyigai, Maina, Sawe and Kipkoimet or Kaberur. In common with other Kalenjin groups the Marakwet have corresponding female age-sets which are Chelemei, Tebesit, Chesyewa (or Kipturbei or Chepturetu), Sigin-gin, Kapture (or Kakiptura), Charkina, Chelyong' and Chemeri. The circumcision operation (*kemur*) is followed after the wound heals (one or two weeks) by the educational part of initiation – instruction in social behaviour, the importance of courage and fearlessness – before the initiates (*sorng'ony*) are welcomed back into society with feasting.

For girls, initiation is immediately followed by marriage. The husband-to-be makes a preliminary visit to the girl's home, where he exchanges his spear and other weapons for her *sile* (a thin stick given to girls on initiation) and then opens negotiations with the girl's parents. There are many forbidden relationships which may debar the suitor from marrying the girl. The totem group, relationship by marriage, or the age-set of the girl may prove to be taboo. A man may not marry a girl from the same age-set as that of his daughter or the daughter of a member of his own age-set, whatever her age-set may be, as these relationships are considered ritually incestuous. There is no immediate exchange of bride wealth, and the girl, throughout the negotiations and on the preliminary visit to the man's homestead, adopts a stance of arrogance and contempt, designed to extract promises of livestock and other gifts. A return visit to her home will indicate that the first stage of marriage has been completed (*kaip chi korgo* – a man has taken a woman). The ritual completion of the marriage can take place only after the birth of children, when the ceremony of *katunisio* is performed.

The birth of a child is a happy occasion. The mother is confined to her hut for a month after giving birth, and children are told that she has gone to the home of the monkeys to ask for a child. The new-born baby is called *cherere* (monkey) and the mother speaks of *chererenyu* (my monkey). The child is named at birth,

Opposite: A Marakwet girl awaiting womanhood at Kamorin village in Kenya's Kerio Valley. Initiation, sonok or tum, marks the entrance of a Marakwet m[...] or woman into adult society. The obligations of adulthood cannot be exercised without it.

the name often depending on time or circumstance of the birth: for instance, night *(kemoi)* Kipkemoi/Chepkemoi depending on whether the baby is a boy or girl; dawn *(korire kore)* Kipkorir/Chepkorir; late morning *(limo)* Kilimo/Chelimo; evening *(kurotu no)* Kiprono/Cherono; mother on a visit *(rutoi)* Ruto/Cheruto.

The council of elders *(kok)* is the traditional governing force of the Marakwet people and may decide day-to-day tribal matters such as an inheritance and succession and land disputes; formerly murder would be judged by the *kok*, with the oath *(muma)* and appeal to the omnipotent creator *Asis* as the last resort when there had been failure to find an acceptable solution to a dispute. Of a dead man it is said, *kawo kap moson* – he has gone to the baboons. Burial rituals vary widely among the Marakwet but all have a common design, to drive away evil spirits *(oi)* which call the living to the dead.

Herbalists *(chepkerichin)*, usually women, were and still are consulted for treatment of less serious illnesses, and they have a vast repository of knowledge of medicinal plants. Those who specialise, particularly gynaecologists, are visited by women from all parts of Marakwet; scarification prior to the application of herbs and blood letting *(kulso)* to relieve pain are the two common methods of treatment. Trephining was formerly practised by traditional Marakwet surgeons *(ng'omut)* who removed the fractured part of the skull, taking care to avoid fatal penetration of the brain. Trephining was also performed to release evil spirits.

The Kerio Valley Development Authority incorporated by Act of Parliament in 1979 is certain to bring tremendous changes to the area, which continues to suffer from severe erosion exacerbated by uncontrolled clearing of the forests and poor communications. Based at Eldoret, the Authority is creating strategies for both rain-fed and river irrigation of cropping and livestock development, exploration and exploitation of minerals and regeneration of vegetation and the introduction of new species of grasses and trees to rehabilitate the environment.

Above: A Marakwet woman on her way to till the stone-fields, barap koi, *of the Kerio escarpment, whic have poor crop yields. When the rains fail the Marakw make offerings and prayers,* korosep rop, *to their dei* Ilat.

Opposite: Early morning sun bathes Marakwet homestead as a woman in the village of Sigor milks on of the family cows. Until recently, disease and rustler made the Marakwet fearful of cattle herding, so they concentrated on goats.

Mbeere
CENTRAL BANTU

The Mbeere occupy the lowlands to the south-east of Embu District, a 1,600 square kilometre area of dry savannah, thorny acacia and commiphora bounded by the Thika and Tana rivers. The peaks of Kiang'ombe (1,803 metres) and Kiambere (1,495 metres) rise above the rugged Tana basin. The administrative centre is Embu. Although they share cultural and historical ties with the Embu, the Mbeere (62,000) have retained many traditions and, unlike their neighbours, have been slow to accept change.

The Mbeere say they migrated from a traditional homeland to the north, a place they call Mariguuri (place of banana-groves) beyond Meru; other sections arrived from the east, a route that brought them in contact with the Kamba. Following a period of expansion into the Mwea plains and Ithanga Hills to the south-west, the Mbeere were ousted and driven back to their present country by the Maasai. But by the turn of the century the Mbeere had fought their last battle with their traditional enemies, chief of whom were the Kamba. British control (from 1906) ended inter-tribal wars and weakened the Mbeere age-set system that was intimately linked with the warrior raids under the leadership of the *njama ya ita* (war council).

Both boys and girls are circumcised (although clitoridectomy has since been eradicated in some areas as a result of efforts by missions, especially the Anglican Church). Initiates are given an age-group name. There are two age-sets (*nthuke*) similar to those of the Embu, the Thathi and Nyangi, and the *nduiko* (handing-over-of-authority) ceremony is conducted by each moiety independently, although both can take place at the same time.

Elders (*athamaki*) sitting as a council (*ndundu*) used to settle disputes within the clans, the litigants taking a solemn oath to abide by the decisions of the *ndundu*. Criminal matters were dealt with by the *kiama kia ngome* (*ngome* being the metal ring worn on the little finger of the right hand by a council member as a symbol of authority). A fine, of goats or other stock, was the usual punishment, but murder, witchcraft or habitual stealing were punishable by death: sorcerers, for instance, were tied in dry banana leaves and burned.

Much of Mbeere country remains an ideal habitat for many types of wildlife, especially buffalo, rhinoceros and elephant, although since the early 1970s elephant have been heavily poached for their ivory. Skilled hunters and bowmen, the Mbeere themselves prepare, or obtain from the Kamba, the virulent arrow poisons they use in the hunt. It was this trade in ivory and rhinoceros horn that first brought the Mbeere into contact with the Swahili and Arab slave caravans of the nineteenth century, and later encouraged avaricious freebooters such as Gibbons (arrested by Captain Meinertzhagen of the (then) King's African Rifles in 1904) to ravage the Mbeere and Embu countryside.

The Mbeere were skilled blacksmiths, obtaining their iron from alluvial sands in the Kithunthiiri area. The workshops (*iganda*) were equipped with simple skin bellows and crude hammers, chisels and pliers. Spears, arrow-heads, axes and knives were fashioned, as well as fine chains, bells and ear-rings for the decoration of both men and women.

Traditionally the Mbeere lived in small, isolated settlements and used digging sticks to cultivate their fields of millet and cow-peas. New crops, especially hybrid maize, Mexico 142 beans, sugar cane and bananas are now popular; cotton and tobacco provide a useful cash income. Cattle, sheep and more especially goats are the basis of an important livestock industry. Bee-keeping is practised, honeycombs being removed from the log hives at night.

Famines, often exacerbated by plagues of locusts, were once frequent. During such times inter-tribal bartering took on an added importance. Traditional sites for these open air markets (*tugu*) were Kwa-Eragu (with the Kikuyu), Karimwana and Kiuriari (with the Kamba) and M'wombombweri (with the

Opposite: A red-hot iron brands the personal symbol of an Mbeere elder on to his log-beehive, one of many such hives which he has fashioned by gouging out the inside of a section of tree trunk. Removable notched ends provide access for the bees.

Embu). Goats, honey and iron implements were the usual Mbeere goods offered for exchange.

The Mbeere are a musical people, fond of songs, skilled drummers and dancers. From youth to old age there are many opportunities for singing and dancing; herding the cattle, working in the fields or on festive occasions. The *kiboia* circumcision dance of the young men and women and the *muthigi* of the warriors to the accompaniment of the *mugage* and *rukongoro* dancing sticks are rarely performed today. *Gitukia* and *mugari* were the joyous dances of planting time; *kithuco*, a dance of foreboding, followed the failure of the rains and the threat of famine.

The Mbeere's world is changing dramatically. The Kindaruma hydro-electric scheme at Seven Forks on the Tana was commissioned in 1968. Kamburu and Gitaru schemes followed and a massive control dam at Masinga was completed in 1982. This complex of hydro-electric plants in Mbeere, co-ordinated by the Tana River Development Authority, is now fuelling Kenya's drive towards industrialisation. As a result, improved communications and rural development schemes are bringing about advances in agriculture and livestock husbandry which limited land consolidation programmes have further helped. Small pockets of semi-precious stones and minerals offer additional promise of a better life for the burgeoning Mbeere, 50 per cent of whom are under the age of fifteen.

Above: Harvest of gourds stacked beneath an Mbeere granary at Riachina on the Tana river to mature and harden. These pumpkin-like fruit make versatile containers and will serve as vessels for their smiling young guardian to fetch water from the Tana.

*ght: Armed with bow and arrows and slingshot an
beere youth stands sentinel over ripening millet, a
mpting target for a host of birds and wildlife.*

*low: A village press crushes sugar cane for the
oduction of Mbeere beer. Fermented with honey, the
ice is mixed with the seed pods of the muratina tree to
ake a potent brew.*

Meru
CENTRAL BANTU

Eight sub-tribal groups (the Chuka, Muthambi, Mwimbi, Igoji, Miutini, Imenti, Tigania and Igembe) make up the Meru people (840,500) of the eastern slopes of Mount Kenya. Meru District falls within Eastern Province, the administrative centre of which is Embu. The coming of the European early this century ended the frequent inter-tribal conflict between these ethnically and culturally diverse people, and the concept of a Meru corporate identity is a fairly recent phenomenon.

The Meru account for occupation of their present lands by claiming that long ago they were held in bondage by a people who dwelt on the other side of a great stretch of water termed *Mbwa*. They escaped from oppression by crossing a river into their present home – and those who crossed at night, the *Njiru* (black people), and those who crossed at sunrise, the *Ntune* (red people), and those who crossed in daylight, the *Njeru* (white people), gave rise to the three groupings into which the Meru clans (*mwiriga*, pl. *miiriga*) are divided. Within a clan influential elders (*agambi*) chosen for their wisdom and skill in debate were leaders in all matters. Chuka oral tradition indicates that they were a people of the plains, like the Kikuyu to the west of Mount Kenya, who invaded the forests and spread through them and started cultivation. The original forest inhabitants were the small-statured Gumba or Athi. The Chuka preceded the other Meru ethnic groups in the area. Differences in weapons – Meru weapons were patterned on those of the Maasai, but the Chuka shield of hide was longer and narrower in design, and the even narrower wooden parrying shield and stave was unique in Kenya – and material culture lend support to this belief.

Traditional crafts of the Meru are extensive. Pottery was and still is an important industry, the pots being built up in two sections and joined round the centre-line. The guilds of women potters of the northern groups manufacture pots of a better quality and greater aesthetic appeal than the Chuka and Muthambi. Pottery nozzles are used to tip the bellows used by the smiths who forge iron ornaments, knives and weapons. A discarded pottery nozzle is thought to be a potent charm. Hides are pegged out and dried, the hair shaved off, and rubbed smooth with a stone. Fat is then applied to make them pliable. Bead and cowrie shell work decorate the garments of the women. Horn and ivory bracelets and wooden and bone snuff-boxes are also manufactured. Decorated four-legged stools are carved from a single piece of wood, and bee-hives and mortars for the grinding of maize are made from a single length of tree-trunk. Fibre baskets, used for a variety of purposes and often woven by the women on the way to the fields or market, are decorated with bands of colour obtained from vegetable dyes. Plaited grass sleeping-mats are also made by the women.

Formerly, Meru social organisation was much like the Kikuyu, a system of age-groups based on initiation. Age-sets over an eleven-to-sixteen-year period were grouped into generation-sets (*nthuki*), comprising among the Imenti, for example, ritual elders, ruling elders, junior elders, warriors and older boys. As a new age-set was created, the ruling set handed over power to the succeeding set at the *ntuiko* ceremony. The population as a whole was divided into two moieties whose age-sets overlapped so that the *ntuiko* handing-over ceremony occurred at a different time in each division. Selected elders chosen for their wisdom and influence in the council of elders (*kiama*) made up the *Areki, Njuuri Nceke* and *Njuuri Mpingiri* secret councils, the final tribal authority and custodians of Meru customs and traditions. Deliberations of the indigenous tribunal (*kagita*) were held in the greatly feared *nyumba ya kagita*. The *kagita* was composed of the most renowned *njuuri* and, among the Chuka, Imenti, Igembe and Tharaka, the hereditary ritual expert (*mogwe*).

Among the Tigania, immediately after clitoridectomy a girl initiate used to go into seclusion for up to two years accompanied by an older woman who

Above: Chuka woodcarver shaping spoons and other implements for sale in nearby markets.

Opposite: Hanging granary keeps harvested maize safe from rodents and forms bountiful larder. The cobs' sheaths provide protection against rain.

instructed her in the behaviour and duties of her future life as a married woman. An elaborate charcoal-blackened skin dress decorated with cowrie shells and coloured seeds and a fringe of fine metal chains (*gitaita*) worn across the eyes proclaimed her status. Once her period of seclusion was completed she would be married. Seclusion and a pretence of helplessness also characterised the initiation of a girl among the Imenti, although the initiate's costume was ochre-red but no less elaborate. The Chuka period of initiation appears to have been much shorter, three to six months' seclusion in a special hut (*gichiere*). If the girl wished to move outside the hut she had first to cover herself from head to foot in a skin cloak. Clitoridectomy is still common, although discouraged by the Government; initiates receive only cursory instruction and no longer go into seclusion.

A typical Meru 'village' consisted of the homesteads of a joint family of up to three generations; married sons commonly established their own homesteads on their father's holding. Wives would each have their own hut and cultivate their separate gardens while the unmarried men would occupy the 'bachelors' hut' (*ngaaro*) where they were able to entertain and have pre-marital sexual relations with the young girls. Villagisation brought about as a result of the Mau Mau Emergency (1952–9), land consolidation and the issue of individual title deeds have since resulted in the establishment of single family units on well-demarcated small-holdings.

The region has good soil and abundant rainfall; tea, coffee, pyrethrum, maize and potatoes are grown in the higher areas, while at the lower levels cotton and tobacco combine to make it one of Kenya's most agriculturally advanced regions. A profitable cash crop is *miraa (khat)*, a mild stimulant much favoured by the Somali of north-eastern Kenya and Somalia. Grown in the Nyambeni range of mountains, *miraa* is big business. Four-wheel-drive vehicles and light aircraft are deployed to rush the bundles of fresh twigs and leaves to markets in Nairobi, in northern Kenya and across the border into Somalia. Grade cattle and improved strains of small stock are kept and many of the well-managed cooperative societies in recent years have bought out large-scale European coffee plantations and ranches in Laikipia and elsewhere and have invested in office developments and property in Nairobi.

Mijikenda

EASTERN BANTU

The nine tribes of the coastal hinterland which make up the Mijikenda, often also collectively referred to as the Nyika, comprise the Giriama, Digo, Duruma, Chonyi, Jibana, Ribe, Kambe, Rabai and Kauma (733,000). They share a common linguistic, cultural and historical heritage. Occupying the Kilifi District in the northern part of Mijikenda territory, the Giriama are the largest of the sub-tribes, followed by the Duruma, Digo, Chonyi and Rabai. The other Mijikenda peoples number only a few thousand each.

Legend has it that as a result of invasion by the more warlike Oromo, the Mijikenda migrated to fortified hilltop villages (*kaya*) from the Shungwaya area, probably in the late sixteenth or early seventeenth century. In common with many of Kenya's people, the Mijikenda – who speak a separate dialect of the same language, closely related to Swahili and Pokomo – only developed a corporate identity in the 1940s. Although they dispersed from their *kaya* a century or more ago, the Mijikenda still identify with them and return to fulfil certain ritual obligations. The original *kaya* were clearings, often in dense forest, with the meeting house (*moro*) of the elders (*kambi*) in the centre and clan houses (*lwanda*), surrounded in turn by the huts of individual members, around the perimeter. Protection of the *kaya* was provided by the *fingo*, a pot full of different medicines brought originally from Shungwaya and buried in an uncleared area around the meeting house of the elders. Here, too, in the *moro*, was hidden the *mwanza m'kulu* drum used at initiation.

Each *kaya* was composed of a cluster of four to six clans, each of which was further divided into groups whose members cooperated in daily activities and social obligations such as marriages and funerals. The men of the *kaya* were circumcised and initiated on a sub-*rika* basis every four years. Thirteen such sub-*rika* composed the full *rika* and when all had served as senior elders the next *rika* succeeded to power.

Specialised areas of knowledge and medicine were controlled by secret societies, membership of which was strictly controlled and entrance gained only after payment of the appropriate fee. Membership of the *Gohu* society was restricted to married men of substantial wealth; *Gohu* members were allowed to wear a buffalo horn armlet (*luvoo*) and were buried wrapped in an ox hide inside a wooden coffin with a carved wooden marker (*kigango*) placed over the grave. Each of these societies depended for its influence on its control of specialised and greatly feared oaths, the ultimate sanction against offenders.

The lower slopes of the hillsides of the *kaya* were used for cultivation; patches of virgin woodland would be cleared and planted for a few seasons before being abandoned. Traditional crops of the Mijikenda include sorghum (*mtama*), beans, cassava, sweet potatoes, yams, millet (*mawele*) and eleusine (*wimbi*), and castor oil seeds. Maize and coconut palms, both well established by the nineteenth century, transformed the economy of the Mijikenda. Cashews are an important modern cash crop. A few goats, sheep and chickens are kept for domestic consumption, and an increasing number of cattle, especially in the drier ranching country of the inland plateau to the west.

Straddling the trade routes into the interior, the Mijikenda were well situated to dominate trade with their neighbours, most significantly with the Swahili of Mombasa and Vanga, whom they supplied with grain and other agricultural produce. Ivory, rhino horn, copal and cattle from the interior, which were bartered with the Wata, Kamba and Oromo in exchange for tobacco, beads, wire and cloth from the coast, were also important. But this symbiotic trade link with the Swahili accelerated the dispersal of the Mijikenda from the traditional *kaya*. Mariakani and Rabai were early market centres of this trade.

The rise of Zanzibar resulted in a complementary and growing interest by European traders and missionaries in the East African mainland, and the first mission stations were established in Mijikenda territory (Krapf and Rebmann

Above: Kikoi-*clad Mijikenda drummers of the Kenya coast. The drums are tuned to provide a melodic as we as a percussion accompaniment.*

Opposite: Girls of the Giriama group, north of Malin in Kenya's Coast Province, pound maize into flour. A arranged marriage to a man several times their age is often forced on Giriama girls when they are still in th early teens.

for the Church Missionary Society at Rabai in 1846; Krapf and Wakefield for the United Free Methodists at Ribe in 1862, and outstations in Duruma, Jibana, Kamba and Ribe thereafter). The missions had no greater initial success in converting the Mijikenda to Christianity, however, than earlier Arab contacts had in recruiting them to Islam.

In all probability, the Giriama have had the longest contact with the Swahili and Arabs of the coastal strip. A number of factors – opposition to the labour demands of the Arab and European planters, a curtailment of their ivory trading activities, the order to evacuate the northern Galana area to create a *cordon sanitaire* of European planters between them and the Orma, and, finally, the demand that they provide porters for the Carrier Corps – brought armed but short-lived resistance from the Giriama at the commencement of the First World War.

Uniquely in Kenya, the Mijikenda construct loaf-shaped, fully thatched, rectangular houses with rounded corners and a single entrance placed in the centre of one of the longer sides. Thatching grass is knotted on to the light framework from the ground to the ridge in regular overlapping layers. But housing design is changing. The use of mud-plaster to reduce the need for so large an area of thatch is increasingly common. Coral blocks and corrugated aluminium sheeting and palm thatch (*makuti*) are now favoured and a shift to the rectangular house with rooms either side of a central corridor, in the style of the Swahili and other coast people, is evident.

The Duruma and Digo *bung'o* or *nzumari* is one of the most sophisticated wind instruments found in Kenya. A double reed made from *mvumo* grass is used for the oboe-like mouthpiece. A shallow lip-shield of coconut shell is joined to a section of brass tubing which, in turn, is joined to a bamboo section in which there are five holes. The instrument has a bell-shaped carved wooden open end. The Digo have a beautiful transverse flute called *chivoti*, which is held horizontally. Made of bamboo, the instrument is some 26cm. long, and has six holes. The end of the flute nearest the mouthpiece is blocked. The Digo are also some of Kenya's finest drummers, using the double-ended *mchirima* and *chapuo* and the *gandu* (which has legs like a stool). The tray-shaped rattle *kayamba*, made of two layers of reeds sewn together to form a shallow compartment in which hard bright red and black seeds are contained, is an important percussion instrument.

The tempo of development along the coast has been quickened by the demands of the tourist industry. The Mijikenda are rapidly changing from subsistence agriculture to commercial farming and livestock breeding on individual, developed small-holdings, and in the drier areas of the coast hinterland cooperative ranches have grown up to meet the demands for fresh produce from the hotel trade and Mombasa's burgeoning population. An outstanding contribution was made to Kenya's political development in the years immediately before and after independence by the late Ronald Ngala, a Mgiriama.

Above: A Digo fisherman of Majoreni on Kenya's South Coast. Fish, lobsters, crabs and prawns are sold by the Digo and other Mijikenda fishermen to middlemen for hotels and restaurants along the coast and upcountry.

Nandi

SOUTHERN NILOTIC

Second-largest of the Kalenjin peoples, the Nandi began to settle in the present Nandi District (the administrative centre being Kapsabet) in the sixteenth or seventeenth century. Successive waves of immigrants migrated into the area from Mount Elgon and an earlier, still obscure, dispersal point much further to the north.

Numerous sections (*pororiet*, pl. *pororsiek*) resulted – Parsieny, Tibing'ot, Kaptumois, Koilegei, Kakipoch, Kapchepkendi, Kamelilo, Tuken, Kaptalam, Kapsiondoi, Kapchepkeni, Kapsile, Kamng'oror, Cheptol and Kamno – unified by the common threat posed by the neighbouring Maasai and their shared heritage and language. Lacking central authority, councils of elders passed on through a spokesman (*kiruogindet*, pl. *kiruogik*) instructions to the warriors (*murenik*) of each section. Not until the Maasai *oloiboni* Barsobotwo became recognised as the chief *orkoiyot* (ritual expert) of the Nandi in the first half of the last century did a unifying direction of tribal ritual and political affairs become possible.

While the Maasai declined in power and influence during the second half of the nineteenth century, the fortunes of the Nandi (who formerly referred to themselves as the Chemwal) were on the upturn. Agricultural skills and cattle were acquired from the neighbouring Luo and Luyia and, with economic prosperity, expansion to the north and east from the Nandi Escarpment was necessary. Well-drilled warrior units (*siritiet*, pl. *siritaiik*) facilitated these territorial gains. The tenacity and esprit de corps of the Nandi *siritaiik* severely tested British penetration of the area between 1895 and 1905. Users of the road to Uganda were repeatedly harassed and, later, attacks were made on the Uganda Railway. Nandi resistance was only broken in 1905 when chief *orkoiyot* Koitalel was shot dead by Captain Meinertzhagen. Traditional functions of the *orkoiyot* were progressively curtailed, and the last holder of the office, Barserion, was imprisoned.

The Nandi live in scattered homesteads, grouped in parishes (*koret*, pl. *korotinuek*). A typical homestead consists of a circular living hut, the rear half housing the calves, sheep and goats. The framework of the hut is built by men, while the women plaster the walls and thatch the roof. Bachelors' huts (*sigiroinet*), granaries and cattle-pens adjoin the main hut. The cultivated land is usually alongside the homestead.

To the traditional crops of eleusine and millet have been added maize, potatoes, beans, pumpkins, tobacco and, in parts of Nandi, bananas. Today the Nandi are proving progressive farmers, growing a variety of cash crops including tea, coffee and pyrethrum and upgrading their herds through artificial insemination and the introduction of exotic cattle.

Asis (God, the Supreme Being) is acknowledged as the creator of all things, but the *Oiik*, spirits of departed ancestors, are held to be responsible for misfortune, sickness and death. Accordingly, they are propitiated with milk, beer and food. The displeasure or requirements of the *Oiik* are discovered from the interpretation of dreams. Spitting is used to avert ill-luck or to bring good fortune; it may be used as an expression of astonishment, as a blessing and to seal a pact or agreement. When the new moon, a shooting star or a comet is seen, the Nandi spit and pray for good luck. Old people often spit on children when they greet them, and a dying elder may spit in a boy's palm when he comes to wish him farewell. Among the Nandi, as among so many of Kenya's peoples, spitting is a sign of open dealing and good manners.

There are seven age-sets (*ipinuek*), into which a Nandi man is born and in which he remains throughout his life. Circumcision of both men and women is practised. Elderly sponsors (*moterenik*) take groups of initiates into a well-forested area to build the special hut (*menjet*) three or four days before the ceremony. Here, following the physical operation, the boys receive instruction.

Opposite: A Nandi tea-picker on a smallholding near Kapsabet in western Kenya. Tea is the major cash crop of the Nandi, and in the last decade or two has transformed the economy of the area. Nowadays Nandi smallholdings with their tea, maize, pyrethrum and grade cattle are some of the most productive in Kenya

Below: Nandi woman sits on the step of her Kaiboi house, on the fringes of the North Nandi forest. The calabash she is holding has been used, like the woven baskets, for generations as a household utensil.

Opposite: A Nandi elder climbs out of the granary wh his coveted Colobus monkey skin head-dress is stored between ceremonial performances by groups of traditional dancers at annual agricultural shows and other festivals.

Above: Nandi elder with bead ear-rings and necklace.

Elaborate head-dresses are worn by initiates, who hunt small birds with bows and arrows to adorn their head-dresses until the 'coming out' feast *ngetunot*. Finally, before a warrior can command respect in the affairs of his people, the ceremonial killing of an ox, *kirie korokon*, is necessary.

The Nandi have a fund of folktales, riddles and proverbs. Once tossed by a buffalo, a man seeing a black ox coming towards him thinks that it is another buffalo (once bitten, twice shy). A goat's hide buys a goat's hide and a gourd a gourd (an eye for an eye and a tooth for a tooth). Riddles are the pastime of the children and young people as they sit around the evening fire. *Tongoch*, says the propounder, *chok*, reply the others.

Many Nandi served in the Carrier Corps during the First World War and thousands more fought in the Second World War, and joined the Police and Prisons Service during the Mau Mau Emergency. However, the Nandi only belatedly recognised the implications of political change, and their own lack of leadership. This realisation was reflected in the launching of the short-lived Kalenjin Political Alliance (1959). Post-Independence acceptance of alien values is especially marked.

Okiek
SOUTHERN NILOTIC

The Okiek are a diversified but culturally homogenous group of hunting and gathering Kalenjin-speaking people scattered throughout the highland forests of Kenya. They call themselves Okiek in preference to the slightly derisive term Dorobo (*il Torobo*) applied to hunter-gatherers by the Maasai. The oral traditions of the Kipsigis, Maasai and Kikuyu suggest that an Okiek-type people were living in much of central Kenya before the arrival of the present ethnic groups.

Although only some thirty Okiek groups have been positively identified in Kenya, the census figure of 7,200 is likely to prove too low, given the impossibility of an accurate count of a highly mobile people, geographically dispersed. Many Okiek are also in the process of assimilation and speak the language of their closest neighbours – for example, the Maasai-speaking Digiri of Dol Dol. The Okiek include a dozen or more local groups in the Mau Forest; the Cheranganyi, Kipkuerek, Kakimengirin, Kipsanaan, and Koibate of the Cherangani and Kamasia Hills; the Lanat, Suiei and Werkile of the Ol Doinyo Lenkiyo and Ndoto Mountains; the widespread cattle-dependent Digiri and Omotik of the plains; the Loloon and Lalaroik of Maralal and the Masula to the south; the Mount Elgon group; the Kinare and, possibly, the Dundule of the western Aberdares.

The Okiek recognise and utilise the different ecological zones of their high mountain retreats throughout the year. On the Mau and the Ol Doinyo Lenkiyo Ranges, the forests of the ridges and hillsides, between the permanent streams draining off the mountains, are owned by different local family groups. They subsist by hunting, for which they use bows, poisoned arrows and traps, by gathering wild fruits and edible plants and honey collecting. Occasional hunting parties may go down to the plains. Many Okiek groups use packs of dogs for hunting.

Expert trackers, the Okiek until recently hunted virtually every animal of the high forest for food. Elephant were killed with poisoned drop-spear traps, buffalo were caught in pits with spikes set in the bottom and covered over with a deceptive layer of thin sticks and leaves, and antelopes, monkeys, bush pig and other game are still snared or shot with poisoned arrows. Poison for the arrows and spear-traps is made from the twigs and leaves of the evergreen tree *Acokanthera friesiorum* boiled to a pitch-like residue and smeared on their weapons. This poison is traded with neighbouring tribes, as are such small artifacts as wooden stools, skin buckets for watering cattle and leather sheaths for fighting knives. Honey-beer is exchanged for sheep and goats.

The Okiek place a great value on honey, and the bark and log hives are hung throughout the various forest heights to obtain honey of different flavours, made by bees collecting from different species of flowering plants, shrubs and trees. Honey used to be stored in large cylindrical earthenware pots, which were sealed and buried. For household, day-to-day needs smaller, rounder pots were and still are used, although the tin *debe* or discarded food can is now the common container.

Okiek women still make a variety of pots, for storage, for boiling meat and broth, and small bowls for eating or as receptacles for food. This distinctive pottery, with its rouletted design impressed on the still-wet clay before firing with a strip of woven bark, is usually round-bottomed and has to be supported on the hearth by three stones.

The typical Okiek hut, seldom occupied for longer than six months, was little more than a shelter built in a small clearing in a forest; a framework of sticks stuck into the ground was bent over to form a domed roof. This was strengthened by interweaving other sticks between the uprights. Animal skins and leaves served as a covering.

One local Okiek group is recorded as having eight clans, corresponding to

Opposite: Wearing an elegant tiara of cowries and metal chains an Okiek girl in circumcision dress carries her head high. Initiation is followed by marriage: an elder binds a bracelet of grass, sekutiet, on the right wrist of the man and an old woman binds a similar bracelet on the wrist of the girl, as a symbol of their betrothal.

Below: An Okiek woman and child, her dress reflecting affinities with both the Maasai and Kalenjin ethnic groups.

Opposite: Honey is of great importance in the Okiek d... Each bee-keeper has his own mark and places his hive... of tree bark at various altitudes throughout the forest... to provide honey of different flavours at varying seaso...

those of the nearby Nandi (Moi, Kipiegen, Kipsirgoi, Kipkenda, Talai, Kongot, Kipongoi and Kipasiso). The Okiek practise both circumcision and clitoridectomy.

Formerly the Okiek did not till the land and own livestock. Today, through barter with neighbouring tribes and income from a wage economy, they have acquired goats, sheep and, in many communities, cattle. The Government is setting aside land along the forest edges where they can cultivate and settle permanently.

Opposite: Skilled hunters, several Okiek groups still li... in the high forest of the Mau. Once elephant and buffa... were killed by weighted spear-traps or in pits. Along game trails snares were set to catch bushbuck, bongo and other antelope. Now only the bow and small gam... remain.

Orma

EASTERN CUSHITIC

These are the remnants of the once all-conquering Oromo peoples who swept through north-east Kenya to beyond the Tana river several centuries ago and who themselves came under subsequent pressure from the Somali. The Orma, also known as the Oromo or Galla and their language as *Afan Oromo* or *Ilma Orma*, number 32,500.

The Orma herd their cattle along both banks of the Tana from Garissa downstream to Garsen, where the river delta begins to drain into the Indian Ocean. In times of drought they may push their stock far west of the river, and competition for grazing not infrequently results in bloody clashes with the Kamba over use of the scattered waterholes. The northern area of Tsavo National Park was formerly dry weather range for the Orma.

Pastoralists, the Orma are renowned both for their tall, slender physique and handsome, Cushitic features and for their herds of white, long-horned Zebu-type cattle – some of the finest in Africa. Ownership of over 1,000 head of these cattle is granted specific recognition denoted by the wearing of a goat-skin bracelet (*medica*) and an enhanced status within the tribe.

Other than a little sorghum (*misinga*), which is threshed out on a level piece of ground smeared with cow-dung and watered to provide a firm floor, few crops are grown. Milk, from which the Orma make butter (*addano*) and ghee (*dada*), and meat make up the traditional diet. The milking of the cows is the duty of the women, the milk being kept in closely woven, cow-dung-lined fibre containers (*wesno*).

Members of the warrior grade are called *quarba*, but uncommonly among Kenya's peoples, circumcision among the Orma is not performed until manhood is attained, before a married Orma man (*gondala*) takes his place in his *gada* or generation-set. Marriage is contracted with considerable ceremony. To the beating of drums, the bride-to-be is formally conducted to her suitor's house. The bridegroom sacrifices an ox or sheep and, catching the blood in his hand, pours it over the girl's breast and right foot and his own forehead and smears it on the centre-post of the house. This marriage oath (*rako kaka*) is binding and cannot be performed until the bride wealth has been paid. That evening a crowd of relatives and friends will collect and sing of the purity of the bride: the announcement that she has been proved a virgin is greeted with prolonged singing and dancing. Orma men often have only one wife, although the more wives and children a man has, the greater his prestige in the council of elders. Concubines (*sajeta*) may also be kept by the rich.

The birth of a child is an event of great importance. During pregnancy the mother will have been brought gifts of milk and honey (*gumata*). After consultation with a diviner to fix an auspicious day, the father calls his friends and in the centre of his house receives the child in his arms, names the infant and blesses it with a libation of milk. At the birth of the first son, the parents take the child's name, preceded by *aba* (father) or *hada* (mother). Should the first-born be named Gobana (born-at-the-full-moon) the father will from then on be known as *Aba* Gobana and the mother as *Hada* Gobana.

Chief weapons of an Orma warrior are his fighting spear (*warana*) and his half-metre-long, two-edged sword (*sefi*). A warrior who had killed five men, lions or buffaloes was allowed to wear the *malda* armlet as public acknowledgment of his prowess.

In former days, a diviner was consulted to predict a time of good omen for a war raid and the warriors' round, giraffe-hide shields and weapons would be carried for them by boys and servants until the fighting was imminent. Women followed behind, carrying dried meat and jars of beer, to cook for the men.

Death is a time of lament. Relatives and friends hasten to the dead man's homestead, wailing, beating their hands together and often inflicting scratches on their cheeks and body as an expression of their agony, all the while singing

Above: Orma family strolls through village on the banks of the Tana River.

Opposite: Displaying fine features typical of her Cushitic heritage, a young Orma girl enhances her beauty with a display of traditional arm and leg bangles.

Below: Dust rises as blue-robed Orma herdsmen drive their cattle to water in arid countryside.

Opposite: Orma cattle and their herders brave crocodile infested waters of Kenya's greatest river, the Tana, to find fresh grazing on a delta island near Garsen.

songs in praise of the dead man. The body is wrapped in a burial sheet (*waya toga*) and when it is raised on a litter of bamboo to be carried to the grave the women make a show of resistance to its removal. They lament for the dead man: *Ya humnako!* (O my virtue!) *Ya ayanako!* (O my guardian spirit!) *Ya gammacuko!* (O my delight!) *Ya saniko!* (O my seed!)

Their way of life as yet unconfined by the bonds of development programmes, the Orma continue to herd their cattle through the arid thorn-scrub of northern Kenya. Trails cut by oil exploration teams provide stock routes; the former drilling sites often supply a sure source of water. Oil has yet to be struck, and meanwhile the Orma ignore the march of progress.

Pokomo
EASTERN BANTU

Thirteen sub-tribes (*vyeti*) make up the Pokomo who occupy the Tana river valley. These riverine peoples number 40,000: the Korokoro upstream of Garissa and in order of descent Malakote, Malalulu, Zubaki, Ndura, Kinakomba, Gwano, Ndera, Mwina (or Kaluidi), Ngatana, Dzunza (or Yunda), Buu (or Ngao) and Kilindi.

Like the Mijikenda and Taita, the Pokomo are of composite origin. Traditionally they derive from the descendants of Bantu immigrants who were driven south by the Oromo from the legendary Shungwaya, which some authorities believe was located across the Somali border north of Lamu. The Boni and Wata inhabitants of the Tana forests, who probably settled there before the sixteenth century, may have been another important component.

The sub-tribes are divided into two sections (*wakijo*), the nine upper peoples (*watu wa dzuu*) and the lower four sub-tribes (*Malachini*); each has its council of elders (*gasa*) who elect a chief (*haju*), and a sacred drum (*ngadzi*) for ceremonial purposes. The Buu trace their descent from a man named Bvere who had a son Sango and three daughters, Mukabuu (wife of Buu, the mythical ancestor of the sub-tribe), Habune and Habuya, from whom the eight clans trace their origin. The Zubaki have nine clans and each of the other sub-tribes two or three.

Pokomo is the only Bantu language in Kenya incorporating major grammatical formations due to Oromo (Cushitic) influence. It contains many Oromo words. The Korokoro now speak only Oromo, once the *lingua franca* of the Tana river basin until replaced by Swahili.

The Pokomo have no land other than the immediate river banks of the Tana. Agriculture is the main pursuit and the major crops have long been maize and rice. Often three crops a year can be obtained from irrigated fields. Coconut palms, millet, beans, sweet potatoes, pineapples, tomatoes, bananas, sugar canes, cassava, pumpkins and pawpaw provide a rich and varied diet. Tobacco is also grown.

Hunting and fishing are subsidiary means of subsistence. The Pokomo have no cattle, and few domestic animals other than a small number of goats and sheep and chickens. Crocodile and hippopotamus meat were once important items of diet, along with fish, honey and the fruit of the wild palm, *kindu*. The Pokomo are expert swimmers and canoe-men. The dugout (*wako*) is used for fishing with hook and line, with the spear (*yutsoma*, as distinct from the hunting spear, *fumo*), and with wicker traps (*mono*) and weirs. A structure made up of two canoes lashed together with a platform of poles (*sangala*) is used for longer journeys.

Villages of ten to fifty domed, circular huts of poles, liana-ropes and grass thatch border the waterfront, enclosed by a palisade of heavy wooden poles three metres or more high. The raised floor (*kitanda*) of the huts is a precaution against flooding and is covered with mats and skins.

The upper Pokomo practise circumcision, the lower *Malachini* do not. Bride wealth is traditionally paid in fish, bananas, rice and maize, sugar cane, meat of buffalo, hippopotamus, crocodile or wild pig, and cloth; the mother of the bride receives gifts of copper wire bracelets, butter and ointments.

The exploits of the ancient hero Liongo Fumo are sung to this day. Liongo is said to have been the half-Arab, half-Pokomo son of the King of Shaka, Fumo Mringwari. He is reputed to have raised and taken charge of a mighty army (mainly Kilindi) and to have subdued the whole of the Tana river basin and the Lamu area and forced the elders to pay annual tribute (*kuwa*) to Shaka. An outstanding distance runner, he is said to have been able to run scores of miles in a single day. Liongo was killed by a poisoned needle driven through his navel on the instructions of a jealous half-brother. He was buried at Ungwana.

The Tana river was an early centre of European missionary endeavour. The United Methodist Free Mission, following an agreement signed in 1884, opened

Above: Pokomo fisherman on Tana River with fish basket trap. Though the Pokomo rely on their fish catches, more and more are now turning to pastoralis as well.

Opposite: Pokomo fisherman drifts in the shallows of Lake Idsowe, at Ngao, north of Malindi, with basket trap and spear.

a station at Golbanti, a few miles south of Ngao. The German Lutheran Missionary Society of Neukirchen started work near Garsen, and later at Ngao and Hola. Ordered out in 1916, the Germans were allowed to return in 1926, but were interned at the outbreak of the Second World War.

Dissatisfaction at the loss of educational and medical services provided by the German missionaries, who it was announced in 1944 would not be allowed back into the area, resulted in the formation of the quasi-political Young Buu Association. Initially the demands of the Association were for improved educational and medical opportunities. Efforts to extend the Association's activities to commerce and transport failed and the Association was wound up in 1956.

Large irrigation schemes at Bura and Galole, where cotton, sugar cane and maize are the main crops, are transforming the Tana river basin and the life of its peoples. Better communications and educational facilities are further speeding the process of change, as is the influx of migrant workers and settlers to the irrigation schemes.

Pokot
SOUTHERN NILOTIC

Two sections, the militant pastoralists of the plains and the less belligerent 'corn people' of the hills, make up the Pokot. Formerly known as Suk (supposedly so named by the Maasai for the short knife, *chuk*, worn by the hill agriculturalists), they refer to themselves as the Pokot.

With the rest of the Kalenjin peoples they share a common language, political affinity and traditions – although, from intimate contact with the Turkana to the north and the Karamoja of Uganda, they have adopted many of their neighbours' customs. Various physical types are found among the Pokot, perhaps the result of intermarriage with the original inhabitants of the Elgeyo Escarpment, which provided (and provides) a refuge for fugitives from many neighbouring peoples, and with the Turkana and Samburu – whom, legend has it, the Pokot raided to obtain their foundation herds.

The pastoral Pokot herd their cattle and flocks across the waterless scrub north of Lake Baringo; from the Tiati Hills across the Kerio to the Turkwel river and Karasuk Hills that mark the boundary with Uganda. Their aggressive search for water and grazing often brings them into conflict with the Turkana and the Karamoja, for to the Pokot fixed boundaries are an alien concept. The administration centre is Kapenguria. The Kadam, a small group of pastoralists associated with the Pokot, live in this area.

Millet, eleusine and tobacco used to be the traditional crops of the Pokot agriculturalists, who also kept a few cattle and smaller stock. Crafts such as pot-making, the working of iron into spear blades and simple knives, and the making of snuff-boxes from small calabashes, ram's or oryx horns is mostly confined to the hill people. These agriculturalists use three-metre bows strung with twisted gut and a variety of arrows, sometimes tipped with poison. A throwing club, a hooked finger ring used to gouge out an adversary's eye and a circular knife (*akul*) worn round the wrist complete the traditional armament of both sections. The pastoral Pokot carry two oval-blade spears. A narrow oblong shield of ox, giraffe, rhinoceros hide or wickerwork is used in war.

The pastoralists share the neighbouring Turkana's obsessive love of cattle – and each beast's colour and peculiarity has a special description or name. Horns of favourite oxen are often hammered into grotesque shapes, an ox with one horn pointing forward and the other backward (*kamar*) being especially admired. Cattle are branded with clan markings, and each member within the clan is able to tell his own from his neighbour's cattle without difficulty. Another habit, adopted from the Turkana, or perhaps a legacy of their fusion with earlier hunter-gatherer peoples of the Cherangani Hills, is the Pokot willingness to eat the meat of virtually every kind of animal, with the exception of carrion-feeding hyenas and jackals. Milk, blood drawn from the neck vein of cattle, and honey augment the restricted diet.

Circumcision is carried out whenever there are sufficient candidates in a locality for the rite to be conducted; but among the Pokot the ceremonies lack the ritual and symbolism which characterise similar Nandi, Samburu and Maasai age-group initiations. Those circumcised during a 'generation' (usually of some fifteen years) are considered to belong to one age-set. Sponsors of an older age-set support the youth while he undergoes the physical act of circumcision. In former days, a youth who flinched or showed cowardice at this time was considered to have brought dishonour on his family and would be speared to death by his sponsors and age-mates. Initiates remain within a specially built hut until their wounds heal. Thereafter they roam the countryside shooting small birds with blunted arrows until the slaughter of bullocks indicates that the period of initiation is complete.

The plains Pokot have adopted many of the decorations and habits of the Turkana. While young men often go naked, a cape (*kalacha*) of goat's skin (in former times often of the skins of leopards and monkeys) is worn by elders,

Opposite: Two Pokot youths demonstrate how their leaf-bladed spears, the cutting edges protected by leath guards, are thrown.

reaching to the back of the knees. An apron covers the front. Today, a piece of *americani* cloth or blanket bought at the nearest *duka* is the more usual garb. The Pokot imitate the Turkana in piercing but not elongating the ear-lobes and wearing ornaments hooked into holes pierced in the nose and the dimple of the chin.

They also share with the Turkana and the Karamoja distinctive head-dresses of painted clay. The hair is grown long and other hair, from dead relatives, is plaited into it until an oval chignon is formed (today more usually to the nape of the neck, but in the past often waist-length). Dressed with clay, into which little gut sockets are affixed before the clay hardens, the head-dress is painted in shades of grey and blue or red, depending on tribal divisions. Dyed ostrich feathers are fitted into the sockets. A small wooden head-rest, for use as a 'pillow', is carried to protect this coiffure at night.

Expansion of their herds in the early years of this century brought the Pokot into confrontation with the neighbouring Turkana and Karamoja for grazing and water rights, a constant source of friction that the early British administrators found difficult to suppress. In 1950 at Kalowa, Baringo, several hundred Pokot followers of the *Edini ya Musambwa* cult (originated by Elijah Masinde, a Luyia) clashed with police, killing several European officers.

Even today, trouble among the Pokot, Karamoja and Turkana is not infrequent – and there is constant raiding by the Turkana *Ngoroko* (bandit) groups on the Pokot herds, resulting, inevitably, in retaliation. If there has been little change in the traditional lifestyle of the Pokot, current road, agricultural and water development projects allied with closer administration is bringing progress to this once turbulent area.

Above: Braided hair, feather and wide-rimmed beaded necklaces of a Pokot girl indicate that she is a candidate for initiation. Dress and customs vary between Pokot sections east and west of the Cherangani Hills of Kenya's Rift Valley Province.

Opposite: Colourful array of necklaces and coils of brass ear-rings demonstrate the vivacity of Pokot high fashion. Though a Kalenjin people, Turkana influence from the north has helped shape differences in Pokot lifestyles and culture, evidenced here in the hair-style.

Rendille
EASTERN CUSHITIC

The north-eastern neighbours of the Samburu with whom, despite linguistic and cultural divisions, they have ties of kinship and economic co-operation many generations long, the camel-owning Rendille of Marsabit District number 22,000.

The Rendille, known to their Samburu neighbours as the Lmasula, also have a close affinity with the Somali – probably extending back several centuries. The composite character of the Rendille people is reflected in their folklore, which stresses the inter-tribal links and migrations of the past. The Ariaal (or southern Rendille) have a cattle economy and strong links with the Samburu. Long ago, say the Rendille, nine Somali warriors herding camels from a remote camp became lost. After travelling for many days they eventually reached the outskirts of Samburu country. Before they were permitted by the Samburu elders to marry women from that tribe the strangers were instructed to discard their customs and throw away the Qur'an, the Holy Book of Islam. The Somalis agreed – and from these first unions with Samburu women grew up the Rendille tribe. There are two Rendille moieties consisting respectively of five and four clans, the *Belisi Bahai* (the Dibshai or Dubsahel, Uiyam, Nahagan, Matarpa and Rongumo) and the *Belisi Beri* (the Saale, Urwen, Tubsha or Turcha and Galdeelan or Galthile).

The camel economy of the Rendille is centred around large semi-permanent settlements of married men, women and children, where only a few milch camels may be kept, and the mobile camps where the older boys and young men look after the balance of the herds, moving frequently to ensure adequate browse. The large flocks of sheep and goats are shepherded by the young girls. Rendille camels are not ridden, but used as pack animals. The camel – which is watered only every ten to fourteen days – will continue to give adequate supplies of milk, even in the dry season when cows have completely dried up. The Rendille mix the camel's milk with blood: a small knife or blunt arrow is used to open a vein in the throat which, after sufficient blood has been drawn off, is closed with a mixture of hair and camel dung.

The Rendille hut (*afaf*) is covered with woven fibre mats (*eima*) and hides; the fire stones (*kindase*) are on the left of the entrance, and a leather water container (*haan*, pl. *haanan*) is traditionally placed ready in the right-hand corner. Pots (*thiri*, pl. *thiryo*), gourds and sleeping mats of camel hide (*nim*, pl. *niibo*) are the main household utensils and furnishings. The Rendille make water buckets from giraffe hide and, in common with the other Cushitic peoples of northern Kenya, use plaited fibre containers to hold milk and water. Fetching water is a woman's task, and the male pack camels loaded with four large containers may carry up to eighty kilos a distance of fifty or sixty kilometres in a day.

Members of a Rendille age-set are circumcised at the same time; each clan has one circumcision settlement inside which a large initiates' hut (*mingidak-han*) is built. Circumcision is by seniority, and if the youth bears the pain of the operation without flinching his kinsmen reward him with a present of a heifer-camel. Initiation (*khandi*) ceremonies usually follow two or three years after those of the neighbouring Samburu. A year or so after circumcision, an age-set receives its name. The ceremony (*galgulumi*) is performed in one vast settlement built for the occasion on the eastern shore of Lake Turkana. Various rituals have to be complied with and a number of youths will be selected to perform specific age-set roles. Age-set officials, *hosoop*, acquire a potent curse and blessing and if they fail to maintain the prohibitions associated with their status it is believed that general misfortune will befall the people and the camel herds.

The Rendille annually celebrate two major festivals, *soriu*, involving the whole family in January/February and in June/July after the rains when there is good grazing close to the settlements so that the youths in the cattle camps can be present, and *almhato* at the onset of the long rains. Each family provides

Opposite: Rendille warrior working as a goatherd in t Kaisut Desert. Prestige and status among the Rendille are measured in terms of camels; but sheep and goats are especially important for their meat during the dry season when supplies of camels' milk are at their lowe

an animal for slaughter during *soriu*, and the elders witness the killing of each beast and mark their bodies with its blood. The remaining camels and small stock are daubed with blood by the father or eldest married son. *Almhato* is a festival of milk, to ward off misfortune. The ceremony is performed age-set by age-set and vast quantities of fresh milk (a week later, sour milk) are drunk before the final ritual and the removal of the whole settlement to a fresh site.

For a Rendille girl to become pregnant before she is circumcised is a matter of great dishonour, and the girl will often be cast out by her family. In former days, it is said the girl and her lover were tied together on a camel which would then be driven over a high cliff. Rendille girls are married immediately after circumcision, following the payment of bride wealth, traditionally made in camels. The Rendille women on the birth of the first male child plait their hair into a becoming cock's comb (*doko*) which is further embellished with fat and ochre. This is not shaved off until the son is circumcised or the husband (or son) dies.

Much as they have for generations past, the Rendille still herd their stock across the harsh semi-desert and scrub of the Korante Plains and Kaisut Desert, south-east of Lake Turkana. But the schools and hospitals of the Consolata Mission at South Horr, Laisamis and Korr are preparing these nomadic people for the inevitable confrontation with the realities of the twentieth century.

Above: The plaited coxcomb of a Rendille woman denotes the birth of her first son. It is only shaved off when the husband or son dies.

Left: Dismantling a hut in readiness to move to a fres[h] grazing area, Rendille women bundle the frame for loading aboard a camel.

Opposite: A Rendille matron grooms a young bride-t[o] be. Essentially monogamous, Rendille society is note[d] for its relatively stable marriages. Rendille women d[o] milking or herding and thus have time for beauty-car[e] and gossip.

Sabaot
SOUTHERN NILOTIC

The Bok, Bongomek, Kony and Sebei (and on the Uganda side of Mount Elgon, the Mbai) are a Kalenjin-speaking people collectively referred to as the Sabaot. Most of the Sebei, the name a corruption by Baganda of the group's more correct designation, Sapin, live in Uganda. Oral tradition and their closer links with the Okiek groups on the mountain indicate that the Kony were the first of the Kalenjin people to settle on Mount Elgon. Administratively the Sabaot are divided by the Bungoma–Trans Nzoia district boundary and consequently are under the separate provincial administrations of Western and Rift Valley provinces.

The Bok, Bongomek and Sebei claim to have lived on the Uasin Gishu plateau before moving west to the 4,321-metre Mount Elgon region via Suam Hill in the earlier half of the nineteenth century. The Kony formerly occupied a much larger territory, stretching to the north. The Sabaot were harassed and their women and cattle stolen by the neighbouring Pokot, Karamojong and Nandi, so that they were forced to settle higher up the slopes of Mount Elgon. There, inevitably, agriculture largely replaced pastoralism, although they are still owners of considerable numbers of cattle, sheep and goats.

Swahili caravans trading in ivory and slaves preceded other foreigners into Sabaot country. Thomson was the first European traveller to visit the Kony (1883) and early administrators Jackson, Austin and Gedge initiated contacts with the Sebei. Formal administration of the area was effected by the British somewhat belatedly, and further dislocation occurred in 1921–2 when the Kony were moved from the mountain and settled among the Luyia-speaking Bukusu. Many Kony at this time became squatters on European farms on the Kenya side of Mount Elgon.

The Kony were redoubtable fighters and clashed frequently with the Maasai. However, beleaguered high on the slopes of Mount Elgon the Kony and other Sabaot people thwarted raids by the Pokot, Nandi, Bukusu and Karamojong by keeping their cattle in caves. The plains became a no-man's-land used for hunting, especially of plains game and elephant.

Not until modern times and the introduction of the ox-plough and maize have the Sabaot returned to the fertile flatlands. To the traditional crops of eleusine, millet, sorghum and bananas has been added a wide range of other crops, including European vegetables, maize, cassava and cash crops such as sugar cane, pyrethrum and coffee. Grade cattle are slowly replacing the indigenous animals. Men are responsible for herding the animals, but in common with other Kalenjin it is the women among the Sabaot who milk the cows. Bukusu influence is a major factor in Sabaot society and in the economy, and there is little apparent difference today between Bukusu and Sabaot lifestyles.

Social organisation among the Sebei used to involve three units: kinship, age-sets and territorial entities. Lineage groups (kota, pl. korik – literally 'house') were organised in clans (aret, pl. arosyek) and a formal meeting of the heads of each kota and aret in the kokwet council would be called to settle disputes arising between the groups. Good or harmful spirits (onantet, pl. oyik) would be propitiated by libations of beer and offerings of food. An age-set (pinta) comprised three divisions, with circumcision (mutisyet) and initiation occurring at seven-year intervals. Thus each age-set spanned twenty years. In modern times, clitoridectomy of girls, who had their own coextensive age-sets, has become an annual event and circumcision of boys is now on a two-year basis. The span of a pinta is thus no more than six years. Circumcision and initiation among the Sebei redefined the social position of the individual within society and indicated attainment of adult status. As among the Tuken, the warrior age-group has become redundant and ineffectual and marriage is common once initiation is completed.

Opposite: Sipping communal beer through long reeds, Kony women near Kimilili on the slopes of Mount Elg[on] celebrate at a circumcision feast. Such rituals are programmed to fall after harvest, normally a time of plenty and relaxation.

Several scattered villages (*sangta*, pl. *songmwek*) made up the geographical and mutually protective unit known as *poporyet* (pl. *pororisyek*). Each unit had its council of elders (*kirwokintet*, pl. *kirwokik*) responsible for deciding issues affecting the group. Until banned by the British, a ritual seer or prophet (*workoyontet*, pl. *workoyik*) exercised considerable central control over the Sebei as well as over the loose confederation of tribes making up the Sabaot.

The pastoral tradition of the Sebei is demonstrated by the importance of cattle, which have more than just an economic role in society. Cattle are lent on contract (*kamanakan*) for a variety of purposes. Those who have care of the animals have the right to their milk and blood. The *namanya* contract provides an immediate animal for the promise of its replacement in the future. A man pays in cattle for his wives, and makes a gift of a few head of cattle to each. The balance remains his personal herd (*tokapsoy*) which he will use to obtain future wives or to endow his sons and to pay bride wealth on their behalf.

The Sabaot of Mount Elgon have benefited from the emphasis given to agricultural and livestock development and improvement of communications in western Kenya during the past decade. Small-holdings are well managed and economically viable and enhanced educational facilities and opportunities have also resulted in many Sabaot obtaining employment in the Government and private sectors. An inherited trait, shared with other Kalenjin groups, is outstanding athletic prowess, and the best known Sabaot athlete has been 3,000 metres steeplechaser and distance champion Ben Jipcho.

Sakuye
EASTERN CUSHITIC

The Oromo-speaking Sakuye (1,800) are predominantly a camel-owning people occupying the desert areas north of Buna, although the bulk of the tribe is to be found along the Ewaso Ngiro river in the Isiolo District. Today the Sakuye of Merti and Garba Tula are increasingly adapting to a cattle economy and a lifestyle little different from the Boran proper. Those who live around the wells of Debel and Koriante suffered the loss of virtually all their camels during the Shifta emergency (1963–8). The Sakuye (Oromo people with close affinities with the Boran, Gabbra, Garreh and the now mainly Somali-speaking Ajuran and Gurreh) are linked with the Sabho moiety of the Boran.

Legend has it that when they first crossed into Kenya from Ethiopia they were taken to see the Sabho *Qallu* (ritual expert). All the Sakuye people are now domiciled in Kenya. Although no historical foundation has been established for the legend, elders tell of an original Oromo homeland in Arabia. Following migration into Africa and a period of Oromo expansion in Southern Ethiopia the Sakuye peoples, then owners of many thousands of camels, settled initially at a place named Saku (sometimes identified with present-day Marsabit) from which place they took their name. The move into the Isiolo District brought them into conflict with the Samburu and, more recently, the Somali.

Divided into some fifteen or so clans (Warfura, Migo, Harsuwa, Madarbah, Jiriwa, Ilan, Horah, Dimma, Delle, Warsua, Kurno, Mallan, Orra and Yale being the most prominent), the Sakuye of the north, like the Boran, recognise the divine origin of the Boran *Qallu*, although the Sakuye of Isiolo District are now professed Muslims. The Sakuye themselves have no *Qallu*.

The camel and cattle settlements of the Sakuye may contain from three to twenty homesteads, each consisting of a man, his wives and married children. An outer thorn fence (*dalah*) protects the homestead, inside which are situated further small enclosures (*mona*) into which the stock are herded at night, when the entrance (*gar*) is closed off. The low houses (*kofia*) are divided by the *gol* partition into two sections. The parents' bed (*olola guda*) and children's bed (*olola dika*) are on opposite sides of the sleeping quarters, which are made sweet-smelling by the burning of perfume in the *kopafa* hole in the floor. In the living section, the kitchen (*bada*) has a table (*mil-jalo*) for utensils and the family's precious water supply is kept in the *garbute* containers on the left of the entrance.

In common with the Boran, the Sakuye carve many of their domestic utensils from wood. The most elaborate item is perhaps the wooden bowl (*gori*) used for serving meat. This is first roughly adzed to shape with a *goto*, then gouged smooth and finally holes for the rope handles are pierced with a sharp metal awl (*ura*). Milk containers (*okole*) and bowls (*damela*) are similarly fashioned.

Children are named for the time of their birth, common boys' names being Boru (born in the early morning), Guyo (born in the afternoon) and Galgalo (born in the evening). If born at the time of the rains a boy is called Rob or in time of drought, Bonaya. A boy born while the encampment is on the move is named Godana to commemorate the event. Girls' names include Bati (time of the new moon), Dibo (problem birth), Dimtu (red-brown complexion) and Midiga (pretty one).

During or just after the rains, when there is a plentiful supply of milk, a special day is set for the circumcision ceremonies, usually a handful of pre-teenage boys undergoing initiation together. The foreskin of the penis is pulled tight and tied off, above and below the point of incision, with thread (*lilan*). The unwanted foreskin is excised (to be 'kissed' and carefully buried by the boy's mother) and a piece of animal skin (*gubli*) placed over the wound until it heals. Girls are circumcised at puberty.

Traditional weapons of the Sakuye are the distinctively shaped spear (*waran*) and knife (*bilah*). In former days a shield (*wante*) and club (*bokku*) completed the

Opposite: Sakuye camels head for the waterholes of Debel in Moyale District close to Kenya's border with Ethiopia. An Oromo-speaking people, the Sakuye range the dry scrubland south of Moyale and throughout the Merti and Garba Tulla areas.

Above: Elegant in her floral costume, an attractive Sakuye girl waits her turn to draw water at the community well.

armament of a warrior. A bow (*gube*) and arrows (*tiiy*) are used for hunting. As with the Boran, a Sakuye man demonstrated his prowess by hunting lion (*nyech*), buffalo (*gafars*) and elephant (*arba*) and fashioning a ring (*qube*) from the skin as evidence of his courage. The Sakuye possess few musical instruments, the drum (*dibbe*) being the favoured accompaniment for their dances. Horns (*gaf* and *magalat*), bells (*bilbil*) and hollow sticks (*rulu*) are infrequently used to add variety. The *dibbe* are constructed from hollowed-out logs, covered at both ends with camel or ox-hide drawn taut with thongs of leather.

Now, to a far greater extent than at any time in the past, the Sakuye, especially those in the Isiolo District, are tending to curtail their nomadic way of life – a trend first forced upon them in the mid-1960s as a result of the demands for closer administration during the campaign against the Shifta. Educational and health facilities are now available, and the Sakuye way of life is changing quickly.

Opposite: Wells 10 metres or more deep are the only permanent source of water for the Sakuye of the north, where as many as a dozen girls and youths form a relay chain to swing giraffe-leather water-buckets to the surface.

Samburu
EASTERN NILOTIC

A nomadic Maa-speaking people, the Samburu (73,400) live mainly in Maralal and the border zones of Marsabit districts of northern Kenya between Lake Turkana and the Ewaso Ngiro river. Known long ago as the *Loibor Kineji* (people of the white goats), the Samburu sometimes refer to themselves as the *Loikop*. Eight patrilineal phratries or families (Black Cattle – Nyaparai, Lngwesi, Pisikishu, Masula: White Cattle – Loimusi, Lorogushu, Longieli and Lokumai) and some seventeen clans are the major tribal groupings.

Like the Maasai, with whom they are said to have migrated south to their present tribal areas from the north of Lake Turkana several centuries ago, the Samburu have long resisted change. For several decades, following their move even further south from Marsabit by the British in 1914, a policy of *laissez faire* was adopted towards them. Baragoi, Maralal and Wamba are the main centres of administration.

These cattle-owning pastoralists mainly live off the products of their herds. Milk is the principal food, augmented with the blood from living cattle or from sheep and goats slaughtered for meat in the dry season. Certain roots and barks are added to their soups. The semi-desert conditions preclude any form of agriculture in the lowland areas, but on the Lorogi plateau and the uplands of the Karisia Hills, maize, sorghum and vegetables are increasingly grown and large tracts of land are now being leased for the production of seed wheat.

The Samburu live in small settlements of between four and ten stock owners. The low huts of plastered mud, hides and grass mats stretched across a framework of poles are divided into two halves, the hearth (*turin*) and the sleeping place (*ruat*). A thorn fence encloses the huts and each family's cattle yard (*mboo*). For convenient grazing and watering, herds are often split. The flocks of sheep and goats are tended by the young boys, the in-milk cows are herded close to the homestead, and the remaining cattle are supervised by the young warriors (*il-murran*) where grazing can be found. Donkeys are used solely as pack animals.

Samburu not only place a high economic and social value on owning large numbers of cattle, but also argue that with extensive herds they can afford to lose considerable numbers in the droughts and epidemics that would be catastrophic with smaller numbers. Until recently, there was no individual ownership of land among the Samburu. A Samburu allots a portion of his herd to each wife on marriage. Her own children use this allotted herd to build up herds of their own, and the husband uses the remainder for his future marriages.

Circumcision and the initiation of boys (*ilayeni*) into the warrior group (*il-murran*) and later ceremonies (*ilmugit*) are conducted during propitious phases of the moon in specially built settlements (*lorora*) comprising several score huts arranged in a large circle. Wearing charcoal-blackened aprons and ear-rings (*lkerno*), the initiates have their hair shaved and are provided with new sandals. Each initiate in turn is seated on an ox-hide in front of his mother's hut, supported by two ritual patrons, one at his back and the other at his right leg. The operation is usually performed by a non-Samburu or Dorobo circumciser, after which the initiates join together in singing *lebarta*. After a day or two, they prepare bows and arrows blunted with balls of resin with which they hunt small birds to make decorative head-dresses. A month or so after circumcision the aprons and head-dresses are discarded and the arrows thrown away and the initiates are now *il-murran*, allowed to decorate their elaborate hair-dos and bodies with red ochre as a symbol of their new status.

Some five years elapse before the *ilmugit lenkarna* naming ceremony, which signifies the progression of the junior *il-murran* to the status of senior *il-murran*. The *ilmugit lolaingoni*, a further six years later, when a bull provided by the group's ritual leader is suffocated and eaten, signals the point when the age-set

Opposite: Samburu warriors display their athletic skill in a jumping dance inherited from their Maasai kinsfolk.

Overleaf: A newly-wed Samburu girl is dressed in finery and groomed by relatives as she prepares to leave for her husband's homestead. Full moon is the favoured time and even days the most propitious for marriage, on the eve of which the bride undergoes clitoridectomy. As she leaves, elders spit on the wife and spray her with milk as a token of blessing.

Opposite: As dawn warms the Karisia Hills of Marala in northern Kenya, Samburu circumcision initiates return with gourds of water, drawn from the distant sacred lake of Kisima, which will be used in the next stage of circumcision.

may marry and achieve the enhanced standing within the community of married men (*lpayan*). Real power in Samburu society is vested in the elders, who are responsible for community decisions and ritual.

Girls are individually circumcised at about the same age as the boys and married immediately after the ceremony. The bride must provide herself with a special apron, ear-rings, a piece of lion's skin to be tied to her leg, beads, sandals and a stick from the *nkoita* tree. Early on the morning of the marriage, the bride is circumcised. Within an hour or two the bridegroom arrives with his age-mates bringing a bull, a cow and a sheep. The bride's mother removes the posts blocking the entrance to the settlement and the bull is driven through to be slaughtered – signifying that the marriage contract is finalised. The elders divide up the meat and perform other rituals throughout the day. The next morning the bride passes between two rows of elders to receive their blessing and commences her walk to the bridegroom's home, where a new fire is kindled using fire sticks.

Although the Samburu believe in an omnipotent God (*Nkai*) who is said to dwell on one or other of the major mountains in Samburuland (Mount Nyiru, Kulal or Marsabit), they also recognise that guardian spirits (*nkai*) reside in large trees, rocks and springs. Men and animals, too, each have their *nkai*. The Samburu also believe in an evil spirit, *milika*. Ritual experts (*kursa*, pl. *kursai*) through their accumulated knowledge of ceremonial procedures are able to assess whether certain objects or behaviour patterns are ritually propitious or unpropitious. Diviners (*laibon*, pl. *laibonok*) have abilities beyond those of the *kursai*, for they predict the future and through sorcery are able to cast good or bad charms to affect the future. Certain families and individuals, especially blacksmiths who are believed to have a ritual power over iron, are thought to have unusually potent curses.

Unlike the war-like Maasai, whose language and cultural heritage they share, the Samburu do not adopt an aggressive and dominant cultural stance towards other tribes. Instead they place a high social value on a mature sense of respect (*nkanyit*). The cattle-owning Samburu and the camel-owning Rendille have long been political allies, although they have remained culturally and socially distinct, the Ariaal section of the Rendille being a notable exception. Today group and individual ranching schemes and improved educational facilities are bringing about long resisted change. Many Samburu *il-murran* enlisted in the British Forces during the Second World War, a tradition which has since been maintained with many Samburu today serving in the Kenya Armed Forces and Police.

Above: Young Samburu girls dance at a wedding celebration. Though they may take lovers among the young warriors and accept gifts of beads and necklaces pregnancy before marriage brings disgrace and custom forbids that two such lovers should ever wed.

Opposite: Samburu circumcision takes place only after long intervals have elapsed between one ceremony and another. The operation is usually performed by an experienced elder from outside the tribe. Those initiated during the same series of circumcision rites are subsequently grouped together in an age-set, divided from the next by about twelve years.

Above: Senior warriors butcher an ox on behalf of a newly initiated Samburu warrior, ol-murrani, as he celebrates his enhanced status in the ceremony of the arrows, ilmugit lolbaa. Each initiate slaughters an o and with his two senior warrior patrons swears allegiance on the animal's fat, nkiyu. The initiate bre the hip-bone of the ox with a single blow of his knobkerrie and from then on is allowed to put red och on his head.

Left: A Samburu warrior feasts in celebration that the novice has come through initiation successfully.

Opposite: A black-garbed Samburu initiate follows circumcision with a month spent hunting small birds with his bow and arrow. These he stuffs and sets in hi head-dress as proof of his warrior ability.

Segeju
EASTERN BANTU

A remnant group of a once numerous pastoral people, the Segeju number perhaps only a few hundred in Kenya, mainly in the villages of Kidimu and Shimoni of Kwale District along the south coast. First mentioned as the Mosseguejos in 1569 in Portuguese literature by Father Monclaro, the Islamised and Swahili-speaking Segeju are closely integrated with the Digo and Shirazi and have adapted to a typical coastal agricultural milieu. The Mount Kenya area and Shungwaya are both claimed as the original Segeju homeland.

Four centuries ago the Segeju were a war-like pastoral people, similar to the Maasai. They owned large herds of cattle and lived on a diet of blood and milk. Like the Maasai, they decorated their hair with red ochre and wore skins. Allied with the Portuguese they drove south and defeated the marauding, cannibalistic Zimba who threatened Malindi. In 1592 the Segeju conquered Mombasa for their Malindi allies. In their turn, in the seventeenth century, the Segeju were forced out of the Malindi area by Oromo pressure from the north, and settled around Shimoni and Vanga. The latter town was to become an important centre of the caravan trade with the interior, and from the 1860s many Segeju found employment as paid porters with these caravans.

Over the last century the Segeju people have drifted even further south, and today the majority of the tribe is to be found at Bwiti, near Tanga in Tanzania. At Independence in 1963, over five hundred Segeju were listed in Pong'we and Majoreni villages, south of Ramisi. Today only a handful of elderly Segeju eke out a precarious existence in the area; not one of them is able to speak the original Segeju language, which is now used only in Bwiti.

The main social grouping among the Segeju is the *mlango* (clan, social group), which has a bearing on two institutions – *kifudu* and *utani*. A neglected ritual object (*kifudu*) is considered potentially dangerous; thus on the death of a *kifudu* owner there is a formal taking over by a fellow clansman, a brother, a son or even a sister's son. *Utani*, translated variously as vituperative alliance or joking relationship, today manifests itself primarily at weddings and funerals, where relatives demand and obtain money.

A wife's funeral expenses are divided between the husband and his brothers and the brothers and sisters of the dead woman, not because the latter are obliged to help the husband because of his marriage but rather because of his own membership of the *mlango* group. A bereaved husband's additional wives pay as members of the group rather than as co-wives. Weddings and deaths are marked by the resonant throb of the tall war-drums (*ngoma ya mikole*). Carved from the trunk of *mchani* (*Albizia adianthifolia*) trees, these drums have an ox-hide (*kiwambo*) stretched taut and held firm with wooden pegs (*banio*) across the open end. Palm branch ribs are used as the drum sticks.

The Segeju share with the other coastal peoples an aptitude for handicrafts. Palm fronds are dyed various shades of purple and mauve, plaited into narrow strips and then sewn together to make attractive sleeping mats very similar to those of the Pokomo (an offshoot of an earlier proto-Segeju group). Hand-carved combs, coconut graters (*mbuzi*) and wooden stools are in common usage.

Ownership of land among the Segeju was communal, based on the *mlango*. Although marriage did not entitle a person to membership of the *mlango*, in practice such ties seem to have given a person equal rights to the land with the others. Inheritance laws applied with regard to coconut palms, but not to the land, huts and livestock. Coconuts, cassava and rice are cultivated, as is a large variety of fruits and vegetables. However, many Segeju individual small-holdings (*mashamba*) have now been abandoned owing to the drift to Mombasa among the younger, educated people, the break-up of the *mlango* system and the subsequent inability of the remaining elders to ward off the depredations of baboons or to prepare the land before the rains.

Opposite: Deftly weaving an intricate sleeping mat, an elderly Segeju woman with gold nose ring embodies her people's traditional links with the larger Pokomo tribe the lower Tana river basin.

Most Segeju now live in the airy, roomy coral-rag and lime-plastered pole and *makuti*-thatched houses typical of the neat coast villages. Few livestock are kept, other than chickens and small numbers of goats. Some Segeju have joined the Shirazi fishing groups (*uzio*) but only a handful work on the nearby sugar estates where immigrant Luo cane-cutters provide the chief source of labour.

The unpopular Ujamaa village programme in Tanzania halted further migration of the Kenya Segeju across the border to Bwiti and the lure of wage employment draws most of the young people to Mombasa as soon as they leave school. The children, womenfolk and a handful of elders remain a fragile enclave against the complete effacement of the Segeju people by their more dynamic Digo and Shirazi neighbours.

Left: Preparing coconut milk for a coast delicacy, thi. member of the small Segeju group is fast assimilating traditions and cultures of her Mijikenda neighbours.

Opposite: Houses of coral rag and palm thatch, mak. in the background, traditional to their Swahili neighbours, a Segeju elder pounds the great drum, ngoma ya mikole, *to summon a community meetin*

Somali
EASTERN CUSHITIC

Occupying some 150,500 square kilometres (virtually a quarter of Kenya's area) of the arid North-Eastern Province, comprising the districts of Mandera, Wajir and Garissa, these nomadic camel people number some 381,000.

Since the adoption of Islam centuries ago, the Somali – an Oromo people who originated in Southern Ethiopia before sweeping southwards into north-eastern Kenya and then northwards into the Horn of Africa where they interacted with immigrant Arab sheikhs to whose leadership they submitted – have once again been moving relentlessly southwards. They crossed the Juba river some 140 years ago and reached Wajir in 1906, and have subsequently settled the entire north-eastern area of Kenya, driving out or absorbing minority hunter-gatherer groups and Bantu cultivators in their path.

The Somali people consist of two parts, the 'noble' or free Somali and the Sab (Dighil and Rahanwein). The four major groupings or tribal families each consist of a number of sub-tribes. These are the Darod (Aulihan, Marehan, Mahamud Zubeir, Abdalla and Abdwak, the last two groups collectively known as the Telamuge), the Hawiya (Gurreh, Ajuran, Digodia and Murulle), Dir, and Is'hak. A small Gosha population of some 1,850 ethnically mixed Bantu cultivators live in Mandera District, mainly along the Daua river.

Pastoral nomads who own large herds of camels and, in favourable environments, cattle, and flocks of sheep and goats, the Somali are utterly dependent on precarious grazing and water in the arid near-desert regions in which they live. The nomadic hamlet (*reer*) consists of a group of related families. A council composed of the heads of all the families in the *reer* regulates and controls affairs with other sections of the tribe. Quarrels over water and grazing rights, stolen livestock, moral and physical injuries and women are frequent and are settled by the councils, or the elected tribal chief acting as an arbitrator.

Within the limits of Islamic law, a Somali man may possess up to four wives at any one time. Within the polygamous family (*raasas*) the nuclear family, a man's first wife and her children, form the 'great' house (*minweya*) in contrast to the 'little' house (*minyar*) of subsequent wives. The senior wife exerts a real authority over her co-wives (*dangalo*) tempered with a judicious indulgence towards her husband's youngest and favoured bride. Although the husband is the legal owner of the livestock, in practice each wife controls her own flocks. But only men own camels, and at birth a baby boy is given a female camel (*huddunhid*) and the boy's umbilical knot is tied with a hair from the camel's tail. This *huddunhid* represents the nucleus of his future herd. As he grows up, gifts from other kinsmen add to his herd.

Both sexes are initiated. The boys are circumcised, today at an increasingly early age; the operation is not infrequently performed on children as young as eight. Girls are infibulated between six and eight years of age; the clitoris is excised and the vulva then stitched together with thorns, removed a week or so later after the wound closes.

The period after the rains (*gu*), when the pastures are lush and water abundant and the young men in the camel camps herd their beasts close to the hamlets, is a time of relaxation and marriage. A man's choice of a bride has to be approved by his kinsmen – a girl's beauty and family wealth and standing within the community are major considerations – before the reciprocal transfer of bride wealth can be made. The suitor's gift to the girl's family is known as *yarad* and that returned to the bridegroom and his kinsmen is called *dibaab*. *Yarad* may involve the payment of up to forty camels and a rifle while *dibaab* payments seldom exceed ten to twenty camels and smaller stock.

Before the marriage is consummated the husband defibulates his wife. Later her vulva is partially closed and only defibulated prior to each childbirth. Divorce, usually as a result of the wife's infertility or misconduct, is both easy

Above: Modern kettle in hand, but clad in traditional dress, a young Somali girl hurries along the water's edge at a dam in north-eastern Kenya. Though muddy and contaminated, the water is shared by people and livestock alike in this vast region where drought is endemic.

Opposite: Alone in the vastness of the sand-dunes a solitary Somali leads his loaded camels across Kenya's northern desert country. Besides camels, the Somali keep cattle and large herds of black-headed, fat-tailed sheep and white goats.

and common. A woman divorced for adultery is referred to as *wey humaatey* ('She spoiled herself, her womb, her reputation . . . everything').

A highly articulate and politically conscious people, the Somali are united not only by family loyalty but equally by a formal political contract (*reer*). Having no permanent settlement, the men maintain their status and water their stock at the wells by force. The indemnity payment for taking a man's life used to be two camels; a woman was worth only a single camel.

The Somali have long been known as astute stock traders. For centuries they have participated in monetary economies and have a tradition of involvement in both local and long-distance caravan trade. Quick to respond to change, they have benefited greatly from the mechanisation of this trade and specialise in long-distance truck transportation to Somalia, Uganda, Sudan, Rwanda, Burundi and Zaire.

Suba

Suba (59,500) is the name given to the conglomeration of sub-tribes closely allied to the Kuria, remnant groups of whom occupy the Lake Victoria islands of Rusinga and Mfangano and the Kasigunga, Gwasi, Suna and Mohoru locations of South Nyanza. In all but the last two locations there has been much intermarriage between the Luo and the Suba and consequently a diminished use of the Suba language.

Legend has it that the first ancestors of the Suba to settle on the peninsula of land which curves out into Lake Victoria to form the northern shoreline of Mohoru Bay were hippopotamus hunters named Ngaruchoya, Wabege and Gimache, who had travelled south from Mfangano island. Impressed with the numbers of hippo in the area, they collected their families and founded the first settlement among the natural rock caves at Nyangwayo at the peninsula's tip.

The Aba-Mohoru – one of several Suba sub-groups – recognise four principal clans: the Gimancha, Barimba, Kithengunga and Kisaria. Although, unlike the Luo to the north and east, the Suba practise circumcision of both boys and girls there is still intermarriage between the Suba and the Luo. The physical operation today is usually carried out in the pre-teenage years. Formerly, girls underwent clitoridectomy after the onset of their menarche and prior to marriage. The young men were initiated into generation-sets (Aba-Chuma, Aba-Ngurunguru, Aba-Gini and Aba-Nyangi among the Aba-Mohoru). At this time two of the upper teeth were removed and those remaining were chipped and filed to points. Wooden earplugs were commonly worn.

Like other Bantu-speaking people of the Lake Victoria region, the Suba narrate how they travelled to the area from Western Uganda, moving eastward, then to the south, around the lake shore. The Suba, with the exception of the agriculturalists of Suna location, were hunters and fisherfolk. They hunted hippo for meat and fat, fished, grew millet, sweet potatoes, pumpkins and, more recently, cassava, around their lake-shore homesteads. Goats and a few sheep and cattle were their meagre livestock.

Hippos were hunted at night, when they came out of the water to graze. Singly or in pairs, the Suba hunters would stealthily approach from down-wind and plunge their harpoons into the selected animal. To the head of the harpoon was tied a long, strong rope and a marker of buoyant wood which detached itself from the haft when it struck. The enraged, wounded animal would plunge back into the water but in the morning the Suba would return in strong, specially constructed canoes to locate the marker. The harpoon rope would be hauled in and when the hippopotamus, weakened by loss of blood, surfaced to breathe it would be killed with additional harpoons and spear thrusts. Occasionally, very skilled and daring canoeists would harpoon hippo in the water during the day.

Hippo teeth were used for decoration, in armlets and necklaces. A few old men among the Suba of Mohoru Bay recall hunting hippo in their youth, and many families still possess a now-rusted, metal harpoon head (*endobo*). It is claimed that no hippo has been killed in the Mohoru area in the traditional fashion for at least three decades. The killing was a time for celebration, for special songs and rites.

No longer able to hunt, the Suba now concentrate on fishing, which provides a daily cash income often the envy of their farming neighbours. Fishing is most commonly practised with long lines of many scores of baited hooks or by drift nets from canoes. A few entrepreneurs employ wage labour to operate the expensive but often highly productive seine nets which are positioned from canoes and then hand-hauled in from the beach. Hook and line from the shore and the basket trap are little used these days, although a few lone fishermen exploit fish fence-traps erected in the shallower water: these form enclosures which the fish can enter but from which they cannot escape. Fish are speared

Above: Suba drummer and child make a musical twosome as father beats out a rhythm on his elongated drum topped with the skin of a monitor lizard.

Opposite: Suba woman drying sardines, dagaa, *at Muhoro Bay, on the shores of Lake Victoria in South Nyanza. Fishing is a male occupation but once the boats have landed the women are left to sort, dry and sell the catch. The Suba have widely intermarried with the neighbouring Luo.*

from lakeside rocks and canoes with the multi-pronged Suba fish-spear (*amasako*) and each homestead has one or two ordinary spears (*erithimo*) for defence or to hunt small game. A bow, some arrows and a club complete the traditional weapons of the warrior.

Canoes play a prime role. The Suba are skilled boat-builders and their products are in great demand among the neighbouring Luo. Formerly of rough-hewn planks sewn together with fibre made from tree bark and caulked with banana-fibre, the small *obuhancha* and larger *obwatho* canoes of the Suba are now constructed of sawn mahogany bought in Kisumu, nailed and then painted with decorative patterns. However, many fishermen prefer the lighter, more sleekly functional canoes made in Tanzania and often copied by the Kenyan boat-builders. The Suba now use a sail of *americani* cloth, whereas in the past they propelled their canoes with paddles.

Fish, often first smoked or sun-dried, is cooked in a fired clay pot (*ekiriga*), while pots of varying design are used for water (*esengo*) and to cook the staple dish of millet and cassava flour (*enyongu*) which is eaten as a thick pudding, together with fish or some other garnish. Fish is marketed – either fresh, smoked or sun-dried – in the neighbouring townships of Migori and Homa Bay or more distant centres.

Suba men and women are skilled in a variety of crafts, and wooden plates, bowls and basketwork dishes are in common use. More crudely woven baskets are used to transport fish or chicken coops and fishtraps. The Suba are a happy, musical people living in homesteads each fairly distant from its neighbour. Unlike the Kuria to the east who live in claustrophobic, heavily fenced homesteads, the Suba have not suffered from constant cattle raids and their homesteads are demarcated only by a low euphorbia hedge. Consolidation of land has not yet been effected, and the Suba are free to settle and cultivate communally owned areas.

The long, wooden *embegetha*, its monitor-lizard drum-head giving a distinct-ive high note, and the zebra-covered *ekingoma* are the drums to which the Suba *embaganthe* dance is performed. The eight-stringed *obukana* lyre and the *erirandi* gourd horn are other favoured instruments.

Intermarriage, most often between Suba men and Luo women, has led to a weakening of tribal traditions and language; many families on Rusinga, Mfangano and the mainland opposite now prefer to regard themselves as Luo. The influence of the Christian churches in the area has also been marked. Yet, while not unaware of the progress resulting from improved communications and education, the Suba seem content to live removed from the mainstream of political and commercial development.

Above: Renowned boat-builders, Suba craftsmen receiv a steady stream of orders for their high-prowed canoes sheathed in timber planks from the mvuli *tree – from wide area around Lake Victoria. At a lake-shore workshop at Muhoro Bay, a craftsman puts the finishing touches to a custom-built vessel.*

Opposite: A Suba fishing boat rides up on to the beach a Muhoro Bay after a night's successful fishing on Lake Victoria. As its ragged, patchwork sail brushes the water the crew prepares to carry the catch ashore for sale in Migori.

Taita/Taveta
EASTERN BANTU

The people of the Taita Hills, numbering 161,000, include the Kasigau, Sagala and Dabida (the latter divided into the Mwanda, Mgange, Bura, Werugha, Chawla, Wusi, Mbole, Mbololo and Mrughua sub-groups speaking their own dialects). The Taveta (7,676) occupy the Taveta division to the south, along the border with Tanzania. The Taita share with the Pokomo, Mijikenda, Segeju and other Eastern and Central Bantu groups the tradition of a Shungwaya homeland; additionally, it seems likely that there was Oromo and even earlier Cushitic influence on the Sagala people and considerable interaction between the Maasai and the Taveta. The Taita also have links with the Pare across the border in Tanzania.

The pioneer missionary Rebmann made first mention of the Taita in 1848, and the Church Missionary Society established missions among the Taita at Dabida and Sangala as early as 1883. The Holy Ghost Fathers were established at Bura by 1892. The Imperial British East Africa Company located its administrative centre for the area at Ndi (1888) but later administrations favoured Mwatate (1902) and Voi (1914) before the district headquarters was moved to Wundanyi.

Tsavo National Park makes up a large part of the vast Taita-Taveta district which borders northern Tanzania, Kwale, Kilifi, Machakos and Kajiado districts. Much of this area is dry scrub, poorly watered, with the Voi, Mwatate and Bura the only permanent rivers. The Taita Hills (1,821 metres) are topped with indigenous forest, heather (*lusu*), bracken (*muama*) and lichens. The hillsides, especially around Werugha where intensive horticulture is practised, are generally very fertile.

The Taita are divided into seven clans, membership of which overrides territorial considerations. Five of these clans are said to share a common Mangea ancestry. These are the Wasadu (Three People), Wanya (Four), Wasanu (Five), Wasasadu (Six) and Wanyanya (Eight). The Wa-ikumi (Ten People) reputedly had a Maasai origin and the Wambisha (Opponents) were the remnants of the original inhabitants of the hills conquered and absorbed when the Taita reached the area several centuries ago. Lineage (*kivalo*) and clan (*kichuku*) were the basis of economic and mutual assistance groups. Marriage to a woman of one's own *kivalo* and *kichuku* was forbidden, nor was it permissible to marry a girl of the same village or the daughter of an age-mate. Circumcision and initiation were the prerequisites to marriage. Age-sets (*irika*, pl. *marika*) were formed from which age-set elders (*wandu wa irika*) qualified for the elders' council (*wandu wagosi*) which controlled tribal affairs. Diviners (*walangui*), rain makers and magicians (*waganga*) and witches (*wasawi*) were held in respect and fear.

Cultivation of land among the Taita and Taveta was governed by strict rules which required the permission of the elders and the offering of prayers and sacrifices to placate the spirits. Failure to heed these traditional demands, it was believed, would result in a curse being placed on the defaulter and his project. Sacred places (*fighi* and *mavingo*) demarcated the extent of the spirits' domain – and evil influences from outside could not be effective within these sacred boundaries. Taita lore records many instances of death and ill-fortune which befell those who failed to respect traditional beliefs.

Sacrifices were offered to placate the spirits and to seek their help in times of famine, drought and individual problems. Best known of these was *kuora ngoma*: a sacrifice offered to the skulls of the ancestors, collected and preserved in rock caves. It was believed that the skulls retained the ancestral spirits or acted as a medium of communication with the dead. The skull of each family member was separated from the body a few days after burial, wrapped in the leaves of the *mkengera* creeper and placed in the clan cave.

Taita traditional crops include millet (*mvemba*), beans (*mgulu*), cow-peas

Opposite: An early-morning fisherman on Lake Chala high up on the shoulders of Africa's highest mountain, Kilimanjaro. Though the Taita-Taveta people are noted agriculturalists, the beautiful 100 metre deep crater lake and the larger but shallower neighbouring Lake Jipe support small fishing enterprises.

(*soko*), cassava (*manga*), sweet potatoes (*makaji*), sugar cane and maize, grown under irrigation (*kukumba mashi*) or in the upper valleys (*ivongo*, pl. *mavongo*). Commercial crops which today find a ready market in Mombasa are many varieties of vegetables, bananas, mangoes and coffee – the Taita region being one of the first areas in Kenya where coffee was grown. Hunting and trapping plains game was economically important. Taita caravans traded ivory and rhino horn at the coast for cloth, beads and wire which they in turn exchanged with the Chaga, Pare and Usambara people for livestock.

Taita huts (*kiwanda* or *nyumba*, depending on whether they are of round or square construction) make up a homestead (*muzi*), several of which compose a village (*ekaya*). The walls (*nganda*) of the huts are constructed of poles (*kikuro*) set around a centre pole (*mngio*) and plastered with mud (*kizozo*). The rafters (*musomo*) are thatched (*kuvimbia*) with dry grass (*nyasi romie*), banana leaves (*madundu*) or palm leaves (*kigachi*) to form the roof (*kofia*). The floor (*andonyi*) area is divided by a plaited palm screen (*kigachi*) and a loft (*kai*) is used to store firewood (*mbande*). The bachelors' hut (*garo*) is placed close by the cattle enclosure.

Blacksmiths (*mshani*, pl. *washani*) manufacture swords (*lufu*) and spears (*shangari*) and other tools and implements including the hoe (*igembe*), adze, machete (*panga*) and axe (*isoka*). Taita crafts include leatherwork and the production of a whole range of wooden artifacts such as drums (*ngoma*), beer containers, stools, plates (*sahani*), spoons (*luko*), mortars (*kituli*), finely finished bows (*ndana*) and arrows (*iwano*). Specialists prepare the potent arrow poisons. The Taita material culture also includes baskets (*kidasi*, pl. *vidasi*) woven from a variety of fibres for flour and tobacco, and calabashes (*kishere*, pl. *vishere*) for gruel and beer. Horns (*ndereri* and *wembe*) once used to signal the threat of an enemy raid today accompany the flute and drum at dances.

Among the Taita, the Mbololo and Mrughua people keep large herds of cattle, as does one section of the Taveta. Much of Taveta is under plantations of bananas, sugar cane and mangoes, which find a ready market in Mombasa and along the coast. The Taveta also fish the crater-lake Chala and Lake Jipe, both fed by subterranean streams from Mount Kilimanjaro. The fish is marketed in Taveta township and among the immigrant Luo labourers on the neighbouring sisal estates.

In the past decade, the allocation of group ranches has attracted people to settle in the lower, arid areas where livestock breeding is still restricted by lack of water. Precious and semi-precious stones are widely mined throughout the district; rubies and garnets, including the unique grossular green garnet marketed as Tsavorite, as well as viable deposits of graphite and kaolin have been discovered. Geological surveys seem likely to uncover many more mineral deposits.

Above: A stem of green bananas on her head, a Taita takes home the harvest from the family smallholding the high and fertile Taita Hills.

Tharaka

CENTRAL BANTU

Occupying the low, hot plains east of Mount Kenya, the Tharaka (9,750) make up the southernmost people of Meru District. They are divided into five principal clans (Mbura, Utonga, Gankina, Muruguru, Kamurige) and many smaller units formerly occupying well-defined territories linked to sacred trees, rocks and waterfalls known as *ilii*. The Tharaka are famed for bee-keeping, witchcraft and colourful drumming. The area has a harsh climate and few resources. Frequent droughts often threaten famine; malaria and human and animal trypanosomiasis are endemic.

The Mbura (Mbua) claim precedence over other groups. Legend says there was once a loud clap of thunder and a man, Mbua, fell to earth in the ensuing downpour. At the approach of the annual rains, sacrifices were offered in his honour. Another tradition is that the Tharaka are descendants of three sisters who migrated from Tigania or Igembe to settle around Ntugi forest. One of the sisters, Ciambandi, was left there and gave birth to the Tharaka; the other sisters moved on and founded the Chuka and Mbeere peoples. More probably, the Tharaka are an aggregation of offshoots of the Thagicu-speaking ancestors they share with the Kikuyu, Embu, Meru, Mbeere, Kamba and Segeju.

Honey and grain used to be traded, especially with the Kamba across the elbow of the river Tana, for beads and wire. Like many other peoples of the Mount Kenya area, the Tharaka smelted their own iron for weapons and ornaments from river-bed magnetite deposits. Weapons were spears, decorated shields of hides or narrow curved slats, stone-headed clubs and slings. Bows and heavy, leaf-bladed arrows were (and still are) commonly used, added poison being bartered from the Kamba.

The traditional house is a flimsy affair – thatched, but with the sides left open to allow cooling breezes to reduce the blasting heat of the plains. Homesteads are often isolated but may be clustered near a permanent water source. A digging hoe (*gechembe*) is used to cultivate small fields of millet, sorghum, green grams, pumpkins and gourds. The Tharaka keep goats, sheep, cattle and chickens (which roost at night in the trees within the homestead) and along the Tana and Kizita rivers some augment their meagre diet with fish. Grain, especially millet after threshing, is stored in larger wicker and plaited-grass granaries (*miruru*) sealed by a slab of stone and covered with a cap of grass to shed the rain. Maize cobs are strung in bundles on a convenient tree.

Famed bee-keepers, some Tharaka individuals may own a hundred or more hives, although the average is about twenty. Hives bear the clan mark of the owner, and are slung with a crooked stick (*mpogoro*) in well-scattered trees. A log of the *muiruguyu* tree is cut to length and a long-handled metal chisel (*kathoka*) used to gouge out the softwood core. The two open ends of the hive (*mwatu*) are closed with wooden lids (*mpengero*) held in place by pegs. Small incisions on the edge of the lids let the bees in. At night, when the bees are least active, smoke from a smouldering handful of dry tinder is blown into the hive and the combs collected in a wooden honey barrel.

The Tharaka are fond of dancing, to the beat of long, wooden drums (carved from a single log in much the same fashion as the hives and covered at the larger end with the skin of a monitor-lizard). The young men start with a stately procession, chanting in deep tones, pairing off when they are joined by the young women. Unmarried girls formerly wore a bead-embroidered short skin skirt that left the thighs bare. The decorative bead necklaces of the young would be augmented on the married women by an apron, decorated with rows of cowrie shells and beads, hung from the neck and tucked in at the belt – but the fashion has been discarded in the last decade or two.

Clan affairs, as among the Kikuyu, were regulated in traditional society by the council of elders (*kiama*), with the inner circle (*ukuu*) having responsibility for certain ceremonial duties. Joint councils might be called to discuss a serious

Above: A Tharaka bee-keeper cautiously removes comb from one of his hives. African bees are aggressive, but honey is a major component in the economy of the Tharaka and many bee-keepers now sell their honey and beeswax through the Marimanti honey refinery.

Opposite: A bee-keeper applies finishing touches to a new hive gouged from a length of tree trunk. Bee-hive and the typical long Tharaka drums are made in the same fashion from the same material.

dispute involving different clans. In this manner compensation for murder, adultery and theft, and fines for making an unmarried girl pregnant would be decided. Disputes on matters of fact would be settled by the swearing of the *kithitu* oath. It was believed a liar or his immediate family would die. A portion of any fine imposed (calculated in goats) would go to the clan.

All Tharaka men are circumcised at a ceremony before the second, shorter rains (August/September). Large quantities of liquor, supplied by the mothers of the initiates, are consumed. The boys awaiting circumcision drink their share some distance from the clan elders. Girls undergo clitoridectomy just before menstruation commences. The ear-lobes of both sexes used to be pierced before circumcision, and a wooden or metal plug inserted – a custom now abandoned. Close friendship between Tharaka men of the same clan was often sealed by blood-brotherhood, which was marked by an exchange of bulls. The heads and hides were returned to the original owner.

Bride wealth is payable by the husband-to-be. Once it is paid, he goes to collect his bride from her homestead and returns with her to his own. On the way, they must consummate the wedding. The father-in-law of the bride 'warms' the marriage hut with gifts of livestock and ornaments. The bride's mother provides her with new hearthstones from the river-bed and with cooking pots. Certain relationships are forbidden. A man may not marry a girl of his own clan, or the daughter of a man who is a blood-brother. On a father's death, a son may marry any of his father's wives, except the 'chief' wife or his own mother. A goat – a ritual sacrifice to mark a birth or a marriage and to avert ill-fortune as well – is slaughtered and eaten by the elders to purify the bereaved homestead.

The Tharaka are renowned, like the neighbouring Kamba, for their knowledge of herbal treatments and witchcraft (*urogi*). The sacrifices in such practices are usually carried out by a witchdoctor (*muga'o*) on rocky hilltops. His services remain in steady demand; and throughout Tharaka those of high repute are always welcome. Their bags of paraphernalia may include roots, bark and leaves of medicinal trees, snail shells and large sea-shells packed with ointments, calabashes and cow-horns and the inevitable fly-whisk to cure (*kiorio*) patients. The ritual treatment is accompanied by incantations and dances.

Even today, the Tharaka way of life has changed little. Primary schools are ill-attended, communications and roads neglected. Apart from their goats, sold off in times of famine, the Tharaka have few ways of earning a cash income. Shopping baskets plaited from the leaves of doum palms, so common on the plains, bring a few welcome shillings when sold in market centres. The importance of this trade is underscored by the sight of schoolchildren and women plaiting away industriously at all times. Cotton and tobacco are other possible sources of money.

Above: A Tharaka witchdoctor makes an incantation part of the treatment of a sick patient. Many travel lc distances to consult the better-known witchdoctors, the Tharaka are renowned for the potency of their m and traditional medicines.

Tuken

SOUTHERN NILOTIC

Third largest of the Kalenjin-speaking peoples, the semi-pastoral Tuken (often Tugen and formerly better known as the Kamasia) occupy a narrow rectangle of the Rift Valley floor, bounded on the west by the Kerio river and rising to the east in the parallel ranges of the 2,500 metre Tugen and Kamasia hills. The administrative centre is the fast-developing but previously somewhat inaccessible town of Kabarnet. Other centres are Eldama Ravine to the south and Karbatonjo.

In common with other Kalenjin groups of the Kerio Valley, the Tuken relate that they came originally from Mount Elgon region, but probably the sanctuary provided by the high hills also attracted refugees from a large catchment area to the north and west. The Tuiyoi clan claim to have originated from Sirigoet in the Uasin Gishu plateau and the Targok Kapter of Chebartigon have affiliations with the Ilchamus of Baringo. Mount Kenya is sometimes claimed as an additional Tuken homeland.

The Tuken of the fertile uplands (*masop*) have a different socio-economic pattern to those occupying the semi-arid lowlands (*soi*). The intermediate zones are known as *kamas*. On the high forested slopes of *masop*, *Podocarpus gracilior* (*benet*), African Pencil Cedar (*torokwo*), *Fiscus natalis* (*simotuet*), *Tarchonanthus camphoratus* (*lolekwo*) and several species of olive (*kiptakeriondu* and *yemit*) contrast with the euphorbia candelabra (*kures*) and acacias of *soi*.

Eleusine (*pek*), millet (*mosongok*), sorghum, beans, bananas, tomatoes and peppers and other vegetables and more recently coffee and pyrethrum are the main agricultural products of the consolidated holdings of *masop*; in the less densely settled *soi*, cassava, groundnuts, onions, cotton and sisal are grown and the emphasis is on livestock rearing. There is mutual lending of stock between families in *soi* and *masop* as an insurance against disease and raiding. The Tuken of the uplands areas have extensively cross-bred their cattle with improved bulls and dairy marketing cooperatives are well established.

Early contacts with the caravans of explorers and traders, to whom they supplied millet and other foods, were extended when European farmers settled along their southern boundary and many Tuken took up wage employment on farms, especially in the Eldama Ravine area which was alienated for European settlement. The Tuken were also considered exceptionally powerful rain-makers, much in demand among the Nandi. From the roots of the *Acokanthera freisiorum* they extracted an arrow poison containing ouabain (a cardiac glycoside, which affects the heart) which was used in hunting and bartered with neighbouring groups.

Spatial groups include the patrilineally linked clan (*kokwet*) and a larger territorial cluster made up of several clans termed a *pororiet* (pl. *pororiosiek*). A wise, persuasive speaker in the elders' council known for his kindness and generosity is elected as spokesman for each *pororiet*. Clan (*oretinuik*, pl. *oret*) names are Kimoi, Kobilo, Kabon, Saniako, Sokomo, Sote, Talai, Targok, Teriki and Tuiyoi. Each has its associated totem, examples of which are Kimoi – buffalo (*so*), Kabon – baboon (*mose*), Talai – lion (*ngetuny*) and Tuiyoi – thunder (*ilat*). The Tuken recognise an all-powerful God (*Asista*) associated with the sky.

The circumcision sequence is an integral part of the whole age-set system which the Tuken share with other Kalenjin-speaking people, especially the Nandi with whom they have common age-set names. The Tuken have seven age-sets for men (Kipnyikeu, Nyonki, Chumo, Sowe, Korongoro, Kipwoimet and Kablelech). An eighth age-set, Maina, was dropped by the Tuken early in the nineteenth century after they fought and were seriously defeated by the Keiyo. The elders decreed that the remnants of Maina should join Nyonki, lest a disaster of a similar nature recurred the next time a set of that name occupied the grade of senior warriors. Parallel age-sets of the women are Jelemei, Jepargamai, Jepingwek, Jesiran, Jemasinya, Jesur and Kusantja.

Opposite: An elderly Tuken woman on the Kamasia escarpment sews together a new dress of goat-skin outside her hut where gourds hang in profusion.

Alternate flowerings of the *setiot* bush, which blooms every seven or eight years, mark the time of circumcision (*kamuratan*) – and there is therefore a change in the age-set cycle every fifteen years or so. Seven, originally eight, age-sets (*abenuokik*, pl. *ebendo*) spanned some four generations. A child (*lalwe*, pl. *lakwanik*) progressed after initiation to the warrior class (*moren*, pl. *morenik*) – long since rendered ineffective and meaningless. The ritual sponsor, circumciser and instructor of the initiate was a member of the next senior adjacent age-set. The children of a man and his wife would join the next but one age-set after those of their parents. A man's first wife would be of a parallel age-set to his own, although subsequent wives would probably be of junior age-sets. Elders were accorded a high degree of respect (*nkanyit*).

The traditional Tuken hut (*kaita*, pl. *gotik*) was built from a circle, exceptionally a double circle, of cedar stakes set around a centre post (*talakta*, pl. *talakwet*). The walls were mud-plastered and the roof thatched. At the base of the *talakta* was the dwelling place of the ancestors (*biikwok che bo keny*).

The Tuken hold local, periodic markets at which surplus produce is sold. In addition, the men bring for sale chewing tobacco, arrows, cow-bells, walking sticks, stools and wooden dishes. The Keiyo women readily sell their earthenware pots at these markets, for the Tuken have no suitable pottery clay.

President Daniel Toroitich arap Moi, born in 1924 in the tiny village of Kurieng'wo in Sacho Location of Baringo District and educated at Karbatonjo and Kapsabet, is a Tuken. A former teacher, he was nominated to the Legislative Assembly to represent Rift Valley Province in 1955, became Minister for Education in 1961 and Kenya's third vice-president in 1967. He succeeded to the presidency on the death of President Jomo Kenyatta on August 22, 1978.

Above: The traditional dress of Tuken women. Only married women can wear the coiled brass ear-rings, bead necklaces and armbands.

Opposite: A Tuken man leaving the family homestead with its surrounding thorn fence into which the family livestock are herded at night, safe from predators and cattle raiders.

Turkana

EASTERN NILOTIC

The Turkana (207,250) inhabit the whole north-west of Kenya between Lake Turkana to the east and the escarpment marking the Uganda boundary on the west. The administrative centre is Lodwar. The Muruaolon massif in west-central Turkanaland dwarfs the other ranges of hills, with the exception of Lorionetom in the north-east. Muruaolon (Murua Ngithigerr Hills) is some 65 kilometres by 50 kilometres, all of which is over 1,200 metres and the peaks reach 2,100 metres.

The Turkana originated from the area further west. Legend has it that young Jie men in search of a stray ox wandered into the Tarash Valley and there met an old woman of their tribe gathering wild fruit. Impressed by the rich, empty land and profusion of berries they returned to Jieland, persuaded other young men and women to join them and returned with their stock to settle. The Jie and Turkana have been traditional allies ever since.

Turkana are either of the forest people (*Nimonia*) or the people of the plains (*Nocuro*) into which groupings all territorial districts are irrationally divided. There are twenty or so clans (*ategerin*) scattered over the whole country, but the effective Turkana community is not a territorial section or clan but a neighbourhood (*adakar*), the group of people grazing and browsing their stock in the same area. All Turkana men belong to one of two generation-sets: the Stones (*Nimur*) or Leopards (*Nerisai*). Fathers and sons belong to alternate sets, which adopt elaborate decoration procedures to differentiate the groups.

Comparatively fortunate in water supplies, the Turkana rely on three main sources for their stock: rock pools after rain (*ebur*), a few scarce springs (*ecuar*) and the more usual waterholes (*akar*) along watercourses. These are often so deep that several women may have to bucket the water hand-to-hand to the surface.

Men herd and water the cattle, rub their horns with fat and sing and dance to them in the evening. Milk and blood is the main diet, and cattle provide the hides for sleeping mats, to cover the huts against rain, and to make sandals. The horns are used for snuff containers. Camels are also important in the Turkana economy. Goats and sheep are herded by small girls or boys and killed for guests, minor rituals or solely for meat. Donkeys are used solely as pack animals, the hides being cut into strips for panniers.

Dried milk (*edodo*) is made by boiling large quantities of fresh milk and drying it on skins. Camels' milk cannot be churned for butter, but is especially good for babies as it has a low fat content and is easily digested. Wild berries are crushed and made into cakes with blood or ground into a dried meal. The Turkana women cultivate their homelands (*akwap*) near watercourses in the rainy season (*agiporo*) where they grow millet and gourds. Fishing – in Lake Turkana – plays a small part in Turkana economics, being especially practised during the dry season (*akumo*) or periods of famine.

A Turkana homestead (*awi*) comprises a man and his wife and children. Sons remain within the family group, and when they marry their wives join the husbands' *awi*. Daughters leave their fathers' homesteads on marriage to join those of their husbands. A family *awi* is rarely a single enclosure and *awi napolon* and *awi abor* are the names given to the principal enclosure where the head of the family lives and to the secondary enclosure of additional wives and their children and sons who have already married. In reality, Turkana homesteads are rarely built in isolation but in association with *awi* of other families. The main entrance of a Turkana homestead faces east. Immediately inside are the fireplace and sleeping quarters of the head of the homestead, and the day hut (*ekal*) and night hut (*akai*) of the chief wife are on the right of the entrance.

For the Turkana, marriage is much more than a single legal act of making a girl the wife of a man. The three-year ceremonial process is designed to ensure the ritual, spiritual and social well-being of those involved and the fertility of the

Opposite: Turkana children draw water from a hole in the sands of the Kakuma river in the far north-west of Kenya. The river flows for only a few weeks each year during the rains.

Below: A sleeping-stool protects the elaborate coiffure of a Turkana man from damage as he rests during a desert trek.

Opposite: Turkana nomads rest in the shade of a solit? thorn bush close to a precious permanent water-hole. When not in use, the well is covered with doum-palm logs to prevent contamination.

woman and the future welfare of her children. Not until the first child has been weaned and has reached walking age can the marriage process be completed. Considerable numbers of large stock (cattle or camels) are required to meet the bride wealth, and these the suitor obtains from his own herds and those of his father, his father's and his mother's brothers, stock associates and bond-friends. The important position of the wife in the *awi* is reflected in the close ties and links that will be perpetuated between her husband on the one hand and her father and brothers on the other.

The Turkana have evolved a material culture peculiar to themselves. Water troughs and containers are carved from wood and decorated with poker work; fat, butter and milk containers are made from hides (particularly camel) decorated with beadwork and cowries. Turkana, 'the finest fighting men in East Africa', are well equipped for their profession. Traditional weapons are an eight-foot, leaf-shaped spear, knobkerrie fighting stick, wrist knife, finger hook and for defence a buffalo, giraffe or hippopotamus hide shield. The women wear enormous quantities of beads around the neck and a neck-ring (*alagam*) of brass or aluminium.

The Turkana place great faith in diviners (*nimuror*), the priestly *Imuron Akuj* in communication with the supreme diety *Akuj*, the *Imuron Ekitoit* skilled in interpreting dreams, the application of mud masks and infusions of herbs to cure illness, and the sandal diviners (*Imuron akalamlam*) who cast a sandal to divine a course of action or foretell the future.

The Turkana have a reputation as skilled herdsmen and fearless watchmen. Improved communications are slowly eroding their traditional insularity brought about by the inaccessibility of their desert homeland. Settlement schemes based on irrigated plots along the Turkwel and Kerio rivers and fishing cooperatives along the western shore of Lake Turkana are being encouraged by Government and Christian missions. The ambitious Turkwel Gorge hydro-electric and irrigation scheme will provide many thousands of hectares of irrigated land for agricultural settlement.

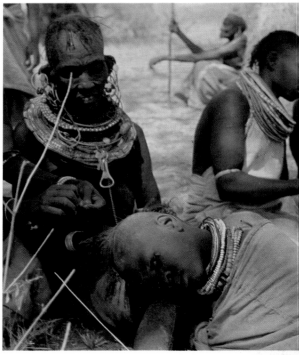

Above: Though they have little in the way of possessions, Turkana women wear a profusion of necklaces and armlets and spend long hours fashionin? each other's hair-styles.

ibliography

ABUOR, C. O.: *White Highlands No More*, Pan African Researchers, Nairobi, 1970

ABUSO, P. A.: *A Traditional History of the Abakuria 1400–1914*, Kenya Literature Bureau, Nairobi, 1980

ADAMSON, J.: *The Peoples of Kenya*, Collins and Harvill Press, London, 1967

ALLEN, J. de V.: *Lamu*, Kenya Museum Society, Nairobi, 1972

ALLEN, J. de V.: *Lamu Town*, National Museum Trustees of Kenya, Mombasa

AMIN, M.: *Cradle of Mankind*, Chatto and Windus, London, 1981

AMIN, M., and MOLL, P.: *Kenya's World-Beating Athletes*, East African Publishing House, Nairobi, 1972

AMIN, M., and MOLL, P.: *Mzee Jomo Kenyatta*, Transafrica, Nairobi, 1974

AMIN, M., and MOLL, P.: *One Man, One Vote*, East African Publishing House, Nairobi, 1975

AMIN, M., WILLETTS, D., and TETLEY, B.: *Journey through Kenya*, Bodley Head, London, 1982

ANDERSEN, K. B.: *African Traditional Architecture*, Oxford University Press, Nairobi, 1977

AYOT, H. O.: *Historical Texts of the Lake Region of East Africa*, Kenya Literature Bureau, Nairobi, 1977

AYOT, H. O.: *The Lake Region of East Africa*, Kenya Literature Bureau, Nairobi, 1977

AYOT, H. O.: *A History of the Luo Abasuba of Western Kenya*, Kenya Literature Bureau, Nairobi, 1979

BARKER, E. E.: *A Short History of Nyanza*, East African Literature Bureau, Nairobi, 1950

BARNETT, D. B.: *Kenya Churches Handbook*, Evangel Publishing House, Kisumu, 1973

BARRA, G.: *1,000 Kikuyu Proverbs*, East African Publishing House, Nairobi, 1959

BAXTER, P. T. W.: *The Boran of Northern Kenya*, published thesis, Oxford, 1954

BEECH, M. W. H.: *The Suk*, Clarendon Press, Oxford, 1911

BLACKBURN, R. H.: 'The Okiek and Their History', *Azania*, Vol. IX, Nairobi, 1974

BROWN, L.: *East African Mountains and Lakes*, East African Publishing House, Nairobi, 1971

CAGNOLO, FR.: *The A-Kikuyu*, Catholic Mission of the Consolata Fathers, Nyeri, 1933

CARSON, J. B.: *Sun, Sand and Safari*, Robert Hale, London, 1957

CHERCHI, SISTO: *I Pastori del Kaisut* (Rendille), ISBS-Castelnuovo D. Bosco, Asti, 1977

CONSOLATA FATHERS: *Elmolo*, Consolata Fathers, Turin, 1980

CONSOLATA FATHERS: *Samburu*, Consolata Fathers, Turin, 1980

CONSOLATA FATHERS: *Turkana*, Consolata Fathers, Turin, 1980

DALE, I. R., and GREENWAY, P. J.: *Kenya Trees and Shrubs*, Buchanan's Estates Limited/ Hatchards, London, 1961

DORAN, K. BREWER: *Personal Art: A Study of Artistic Expression Among the Njemps, a Pastoral People of Kenya*, Dartmouth College, Hanover, New Hampshire, USA, 1976

DRACOPOLI, I. N.: *Through Jubaland to the Lorian Swamp*, Seeley, Services & Co., London, 1914

EHRET, C.: *Ethiopians and East Africans*, East African Publishing House, Nairobi, 1974

FARSI, S. S.: *Swahili Idioms*, East African Publishing House, Nairobi, 1973

FEDDERS, A., and SALVADORI, C.: *Turkana: Pastoral Craftsmen*, Transafrica, Nairobi, 1977

FEDDERS, A., and SALVADORI, C.: *Peoples and Cultures of Kenya*, Transafrica/Rex Collings, Nairobi, 1979

GATHIGIRA, H.: *Mzee Jomo Kenyatta*, East African Newspapers Ltd, Nairobi, 1973

GHAIDAN, U.: *Lamu*, East African Literature Bureau, Nairobi, 1976

GOLDSCHMIDT, W.: *Sebei Law*, University of California Press, Berkeley and Los Angeles, 1967

GOLDSCHMIDT, W.: *Kambuya's Cattle*, University of California Press, Berkeley and Los Angeles, 1969

GRAHAM, A., and BEARD, P.: *Eyelids of Morning*, Graphic Society, New York, 1973

GULLIVER, P., and GULLIVER, P. H.: *The Central Nilo-Hamites*, International African Institute, London, 1953

GULLIVER, P. H.: *The Family Herds*, Routledge and Kegan Paul, London, 1955

GULLIVER, P. H.: *Social Control in African Society*, Routledge and Kegan Paul, London, 1974

HAMILTON, G.: *In the Wake of Da Gama*, Skeffington, London, 1951

HAYWOOD, CAPT. C. W.: *To the Mysterious Lorian Swamp*, Seeley, Services & Co., London, 1927

HENNINGS, R. O.: *African Morning*, Chatto and Windus, London, 1951

HINDE, S. L., and HINDE, H.: *The Last of the Masai*, Heinemann, London, 1901

HOBLEY, C. W.: *Ethnology of Akamba and Other East African Tribes*, Frank Cass, London, 1910

HOBLEY, C. W.: *Kenya*, Frank Cass, London, 1929

HOLLIS, A. C.: *The Masai*, Clarendon Press, London, 1905

HOLLIS, A. C.: *The Nandi*, Clarendon Press, Oxford, 1909

HOYLE, B. S.: *The Seaports of East Africa*, East African Publishing House, Nairobi, 1967

HUNTINGFORD, G. W. B.: *The Nandi of Kenya*, Routledge and Kegan Paul, London, 1953

HUNTINGFORD, G. W. B.: *The Southern Nilo-Hamites*, International African Institute, London, 1953

HUNTINGFORD, G. W. B.: *The Galla of Ethiopia*, International African Institute, London, 1955

osite: Sunset at Ferguson's Gulf on Lake Turkana's stern shore as a fishing crew head their canoe neward with the day's catch. Improved fibre-glass ·sse canoes have enabled the Turkana fishermen to ·loit the deeper waters of the lake.

189

HYSLOP, G.: *Musical Instruments of East Africa (Kenya)*, Nelson Africa Limited, Nairobi, 1975

JACOBS, A. H.: 'The Traditional Political Organization of the Pastoral Maasai', Ph.D. Dissertation, Oxford University, 1965

JACOBS, A. H.: *A Chronology of the Pastoral Maasai*, Hadithi, Nairobi, 1968

JEWELL, J. H. A.: *Dhows at Mombasa*, East African Publishing House, Nairobi, 1969

JEWELL, J. H. A.: *Mombasa: The Friendly Town*, East African Publishing House, Nairobi, 1976

KAMILU, D. N.: *Mukamba Wa Wo*, East African Literature Bureau, Dar es Salaam, 1966

KAMORA, Y.: *Sons of Sango*, East African Publishing House, Nairobi, 1973

KARIMI, M.: *The Arrow Poisons*, East African Literature Bureau, Nairobi, 1973

KAVYU, P. N.: *An Introduction to Kamba Music*, East African Literature Bureau, Nairobi, 1977

KAVYU, P. N.: *Traditional Musical Instruments of Kenya*, East African Literature Bureau, Nairobi, 1980

KENYATTA, JOMO: *Facing Mount Kenya*, Secker and Warburg, London, 1938

KENYATTA, JOMO: *My People of Kikuyu*, Oxford University Press, Nairobi, 1966 (reprint)

KETTEL, B., and KETTEL, B.: *The Tuken of Kenya: A Brief Ethnographic Report*, University of Illinois, Illinois, 1970

KINDY, H.: *Life and Politics in Mombasa*, East African Publishing House, Nairobi, 1972

KIPKORIR, B. E., *Kenya's People, People of the Rift Valley*, Evans Brothers, Nairobi, 1978

KIPKORIR, B. E.: and WELDOWN, F. B.: *The Marakwet of Kenya*, East African Literature Bureau, Nairobi, 1973

KOKWARO, J. O.: *Medicinal Plants of East Africa*, East African Literature Bureau, Nairobi, 1976

LAMBERT, E. H.: *Kikuyu Social and Political Institutions*, Oxford University Press, London, 1956

LEAKEY, L. S. B.: *Mau Mau and the Kikuyu*, Methuen, London, 1952

LE GUENNEC-COPPENS, F.: *Wedding Customs in Lamu*, The Lamu Society, Nairobi, 1980

LEWIS, I. M.: *Peoples of the Horn of Africa*, International African Institute, London, 1955

LINDBLOM, G.: *The Akamba*, J. A. Lundell, Uppsala, 1920

LIYONG, LO T.: *Popular Culture of East Africa*, Longman, Nairobi, 1972

MCINTOSH, B. G.: *Ngano*, East African Literature Bureau, Nairobi, 1969

MAIR, L. P.: *The Bantu of North Kavirondo*, International African Institute, London, 1956

MAKILA, F. E.: *An Outline History of the Babukusu*, Kenya Literature Bureau, Nairobi, 1978

MARTIN, C. M. P., and MARTIN, E. B.: *Quest for the Past*, Marketing and Publishing, Nairobi, 1973

MARTIN, E. B.: *An Historical Guide to Lamu*, Woolworths, Nairobi, 1970

MARTIN, E. B.: *The History of Malindi*, East African Literature Bureau, Nairobi, 1973

MARTIN, E. B.: *Malindi, the Historic Town on Kenya's Coast*, Marketing and Publishing, Nairobi, 1975

MASSAM, J. A.: *The Cliff Dwellers of Kenya*, Frank Cass, London, 1968

MASSEK, A. ol'o, and SIDAI, J. O.: *Wisdom of Maasai*, Transafrica, Nairobi, 1974

MATSON, A. T.: *The Nandi Campaign against the British 1895–1906*, Transafrica, Nairobi, 1974

MIDDLETON, J., and GREET, K.: *The Kikuyu & Kamba of Kenya*, International African Institute, London, 1972

MOL, Fr. F.: *Maa: A Dictionary of Maasai Language and Folklore, English–Maasai*, Marketing and Publishing, Nairobi, 1978

MURIUKI, G.: *A History of the Kikuyu*, Oxford University Press, Nairobi, 1974

MURIUKI, G.: *Kenya's People, People round Mount Kenya*, Evans Brothers, Nairobi, 1978

MUTUA, W. R.: *Development of Education in Kenya*, East African Literature Bureau, Nairobi

MWANIKI, H. S. K.: *The Living History of Embu and Mbeere*, East African Literature Bureau, Nairobi, 1973

MWANIKI, H. S. K.: *Embu Historical Texts*, East African Literature Bureau, Nairobi, 1974

MWANZI, H. A.: *A History of the Kipsigis*, East African Literature Bureau, Nairobi, 1977

NDETI, K.: *Elements of Akamba Life*, East African Publishing House, Nairobi, 1972

NGALA, R. C.: *Nchi na Desturi za Wagiriama*, East African Literature Bureau, Dar es Salaam, 1956

NJIRO, S.: *Daniel arap Moi: Man of Peace, Love and Unity*, Transafrica, Nairobi, 1980

NJURURI, N.: *Gikuyu Proverbs*, Macmillan, London, 1969

OCHIENG', W. R.: *An Outline History of Nyanza up to 1914*, East African Literature Bureau, Nairobi, 1974

OCHIENG', W. R.: *Pre-Colonial History of the Gusii of Western Kenya 1500–1914*, East African Literature Bureau, Nairobi, 1974

OCHIENG', W. R.: *Eastern Kenya and Its Invaders*, East African Literature Bureau, Nairobi, 1975

OCHIENG', W. R.: *The First Word*, East African Literature Bureau, Nairobi, 1975

OCHIENG', W. R.: *Kadimo Chiefdom of Yimbo*, East African Literature Bureau, Nairobi, 1975

OCHIENG', W. R.: *Kenya's People, People round the Lake*, Evans Brothers, Nairobi, 1978

OGOT, B. A.: *A History of the Southern Luo Peoples Settlement 1500–1900*, East African Publishing House, Nairobi, 1967

OGOT, B. A.: *Hadithi*, Vols I–V, East African Publishing House, Nairobi, 1968

OGOT, B. A.: *Zamani*, Longman Kenya Ltd, Nairobi, 1968

OLE SAITOTI, T.: *Maasai*, Elm Tree Books, London, 1981

OMINDE, S. H.: *The Luo Girl*, East African Literature Bureau, Nairobi, 1952

ONWUEJE, O. M. A.: *The Social Anthropology of Africa*, Heinemann Educational, London, 1975

ONYANGO-OGUTU, B., and ROSCOE, A. A.: *Keep My Words*, East African Publishing House, Nairobi, 1974

ORCHARDSON, I.: *The Kipsigis*, East African Literature Bureau, Nairobi, 1961

ORDE-BROWN, J.: *The Vanishing Tribes of Kenya*, Seeley, Services & Co., London, 1925

OSOGO, J.: *The Baluya*, Oxford University Press, Nairobi, 1965

OSOGO, J.: *A Traditional History of Kenya*, Longman Kenya Ltd, Nairobi, 1968

OSOGO, J.: *Nabongo Mumia*, East African Literature Bureau, Nairobi, 1976

OUCHO, J. O.: *The Port of Kisumu in the Lake Victoria Trade*, Kenya Literature Bureau, Nairobi, 1979

PENWILL, D. J.: *Kamba Customary Law*, East African Literature Bureau, Nairobi, 1951

PERISTIANY, J. G.: *The Social Institutions of the Kipsigis*, Routledge and Kegan Paul, London, 1939

PRINS, A. H. J.: *The Coastal Tribes of North-Eastern Bantu*, International African Institute, London, 1952

PRINS, A. H. J.: *The Swahili-Speaking Peoples of Zanzibar and the East Africa Coast*, International African Institute, London, 1967

RANGER, T. O.: *Dance and Society in East Africa*, Heinemann, Nairobi, 1975

RAYNE, H. M.: *The Ivory Raiders*, Heinemann, London, 1923

RICCIARDI, M.: *Vanishing Africa*, Collins, London, 1974

ROBSON, P., and NEWMAN, R. J.: *Mountains of Kenya*, East African Publishing House, Nairobi, 1969

ROSBERG, C., and NOTTINGHAM, J. C.: *The Myth of Mau Mau*, Praeger, New York, 1966

ROUTLEDGE, W. S. K.: *With a Pre-historic People*, Frank Cass, London, 1910

SABERWAL, S. C.: *The Traditional Political Systems of the Embu of Central Kenya*, East African Publishing House, Nairobi, 1970

SALIM, A. I.: *Swahili-Speaking Peoples of Kenya's Coast*, East African Publishing House, Nairobi, 1973

SALIM, A. I.: *Kenya's People, People of the Coast*, Evans Brothers, Nairobi, 1978

SALVADORI, C. F., and FEDDERS, A.: *Maasai*, Collins, London, 1973

SANKAN, S. S.: *The Maasai*, East African Literature Bureau, Nairobi, 1971

SELIGMAN, C. G.: *Races of Africa*, Oxford University Press, London, 1966

SHARMAN, M.: *Kenya's People, People of the Plains*, Evans Brothers, Nairobi, 1978

SPEAR, T. T.: *The Kaya Complex: A History of the Mijikenda Peoples of the Kenya Coast to 1900*, Kenya Literature Bureau, Nairobi, 1978

SPENCER, P.: *The Samburu*, Routledge and Kegan Paul, London, 1965

SPENCER, P.: *Nomads in Alliance*, Oxford University Press, London, 1973

STILES, D.: 'The Boni: Problems of a Hunting-gathering People', *Africana* 8 (2), Marketing and Publishing, Nairobi, 1981

STILES, D.: 'Hunters of the Northern East African Coast: Origins and Historical Processes', *Africa* 51(4), London, 1981

SUTTON, G. E. J.: *The East African Coast*, East African Publishing House, Nairobi, 1966

SWELL, S. G.: *Nandi Customary Law*, East African Literature Bureau, Nairobi, 1954

TANNER, R. E. S.: *Transition in African Beliefs*, Maryknoll Publications, New York, 1967

TOWEETT, T.: *Oral Traditional History of the Kipsigis*, Kenya Literature Bureau, Nairobi, 1979

TOWEETT, T.: *A Study of Kalenjin Linguistics*, Kenya Literature Bureau, Nairobi, 1979

WAGNER, G.: *The Bantu of Western Kenya*, Oxford University Press, London, 1949

WAKO, D. M.: *Akabaluyia Bemumbo*, East African Literature Bureau, Nairobi, 1965

WARNER, A.: *Myths and Legends of the Bantu*, Harrap, London, 1933

WEBSTER, J. B.: *The Iteso during the Asonya*, East African Publishing House, Nairobi, 1973

WERE, G. S.: *A History of the Abaluyia of Western Kenya 1500–1930*, East African Publishing House, Nairobi, 1967

WESTERMANN, D., and WARD, I. D. C.: *Practical Phonetics for Students of African Languages*, International African Institute, London, 1933

WILDING, R.: *Swahili Culture*, The Lamu Society, Nairobi, 1976

WIPER, A.: *Rural Rebels*, Oxford University Press, Nairobi, 1977

WORTHINGTON, S., and WORTHINGTON, E. B.: *Inland Waters of Africa*, Macmillan, London, 1933

Note:

Azania (edited by N. Chittick) is the journal of the British Institute in Eastern Africa.

Hadithi (edited by B. A. Ogot) contains the published proceedings of the annual conferences of the Historical Association of Kenya.

Ngano (edited by B. G. McIntosh) consists of collected studies in traditional and modern East African history published by the Department of History, University of Nairobi.